"In a time when childhood has many detrimental intrusions, this enlightening book offers teachers and parents of young children a new approach to the use of stories... Dr. Woodard and Carri Milch have given us a wealthy resource to address the world of make-believe and play. A must-have book for keeping the wonder in childhood."

—*Christine Ellington-Rowe, Adjunct Instructor for the State University of New York Empire State College, Executive Director of the University at Buffalo Child Care Center, and experienced early childhood professional*

"*Make-Believe Play and Story-based Drama in Early Childhood: Let's Pretend!* is a jewel, an all-inclusive must-have that provides teachers, student teachers, and parents with step-by-step strategies to implement make-believe, story pretending, and dramatization in early education classrooms. Through theory, practical application, and instructive vignettes woven into one idea-packed manual, teachers have a go-to tool box that supports classrooms rich in opportunities for literacy-based learning."

—*Judy Piskun, Associate Professor and Director of Internships, Villa Maria College, New York*

"Teachers of young children who are exasperated by their students' limited ability to express themselves should read *Let's Pretend!*. This book explains why this is happening and what to do about it. It empowers teachers with a background knowledge of child development and offers many fun activities designed to promote language and literacy skills that can be easily implemented in the classroom."

—*Stephanie Gregorie, Elementary Education Teacher, Supervisor, Principal, and Educational Consultant*

Make-Believe Play and Story-Based Drama in Early Childhood

of related interest

The Creation of Imaginary Worlds
The Role of Art, Magic and Dreams in Child Development
Claire Golomb
ISBN 978 1 84905 852 0
eISBN 978 0 85700 411 6

Creative Coping Skills for Children
Emotional Support through Arts and Crafts Activities
Bonnie Thomas
ISBN 978 1 84310 921 1
eISBN 978 184642 954 5

The Yellow Book of Games and Energizers
Playful Group Activities for Exploring Identity, Community, Emotions and More!
Jayaraja and Erwin Tielemans
ISBN 978 1 84905 192 7
eISBN 978 0 85700 432 1

Dramatherapy and Family Therapy in Education
Essential Pieces of the Multi-Agency Jigsaw
Penny McFarlane and Jenny Harvey
Foreword by Sue Jennings
ISBN 978 1 84905 216 0
eISBN 978 0 85700 451 2

Arts Therapies in Schools
Research and Practice
Edited by Vicky Karkou
ISBN 978 1 84310 633 3
eISBN 978 0 85700 209 9

Story Drama in the Special Needs Classroom
Step-by-Step Lesson Plans for Teaching through Dramatic Play
Jessica Perich Carleton
ISBN 978 1 84905 859 9
eISBN 978 0 85700 469 7

Social Skills, Emotional Growth and Drama Therapy
Inspiring Connection on the Autism Spectrum
Lee R. Chasen
Foreword by Robert J. Landy
ISBN 978 1 84905 840 7
eISBN 978 0 85700 345 4

Make-Believe Play and Story-Based Drama in Early Childhood

Let's Pretend!

CAROL WOODARD WITH CARRI MILCH ✳ **ILLUSTRATED BY SUZANNE MAIR**

Jessica Kingsley *Publishers*
London and Philadelphia

'Broom Balancing' on p.70 has been reproduced from Stilts, Somersaults, and Headstands by Kathleen Fraser. Copyright © 1968 Kathleen Fraser. Used by permission of Marian Reiner for the author.

First published in 2012
by Jessica Kingsley Publishers
116 Pentonville Road
London N1 9JB, UK
and
400 Market Street, Suite 400
Philadelphia, PA 19106, USA

www.jkp.com

Copyright © Carol Woodard with Carri Milch 2012
Illustrations copyright © Suzanne Mair 2012

Library of Congress Cataloging in Publication Data
A CIP catalog record for this book is available from the Library of Congress

British Library Cataloguing in Publication Data
A CIP catalogue record for this book is available from the British Library

ISBN 978 1 84905 899 5
eISBN 978 0 85700 639 4

Printed and bound in Great Britain

To our students, both young children and adults

ACKNOWLEDGEMENTS

We would like to especially thank Chris Ellington-Rowe for her expert review of our manuscript along with the many dedicated early childhood educators who have inspired this work including Nadine Hirsch, Stephanie Gregorie, Clare Edson, Judy Piskun, Rebecca Wojcik, Jamie Gregory, as well as Marion Canedo and Grace Schaefer. Our thanks too, to our supportive husbands Ralph and Phil.

CONTENTS

Part 1

STORY PRETENDING AND DRAMA

Chapter 1

INTRODUCTION

Young children love to pretend! They enjoy slipping into the role of the family cat, grandmother, or a mailperson, and through these imaginary experiences gain a broader understanding of how the world around them operates. Using make-believe, children "play a story" and enter the stimulating adult world by imitating it and imaging different story possibilities that meet their needs. When pretending, children use language and actions to represent ideas, feelings, and events from life that are not really happening or present. The child clutches a fist to his/her ear and says, "Hello, Hello," using the fist as a symbol to represent the idea of a telephone. Pretending introduces young children to the use of symbols and signs which they will encounter and need later in learning.

Pretend or make-believe play is part of a stage in the developmental sequence of children's play behavior which emerges at about two years, peaks about five years, and starts to fade about six or seven years as interest in games with rules emerges. During the preschool and early primary years, when children's interest is naturally at its height, pretend play can be a highly effective teaching tool (Pellegrini and Galda 1991). How make-believe play is used in the classroom is based on the developmental levels, needs, and interests of the children involved. Early childhood educators who are able to guide children's enthusiasm for make-believe into appropriate classroom experiences find it an invaluable asset in learning. Often, however, in the complex and challenging world of teaching, the use of pretending and drama can be overlooked or its benefits unrecognized. Although pretending does occur randomly in the classroom, planning a more sequential approach to pretend play assures its consistent use.

This book details three different but related types of pretending or make-believe play to interweave through the school year, beginning with *dramatic play*, continuing with *drama in everyday activities*, and culminating with informal *story dramatizations*. Podlozny (2000) notes that there are no set definitions for the profusion of terms used to describe "drama" in the early childhood literature (e.g. creative dramatics, fantasy play, thematic play, reenactments). To avoid confusion, the following overview describes the three kinds of drama featured in this work.

USING STORY PRETENDING AND DRAMA
Dramatic play

The term "dramatic play" refers to play in which two or more children assume pretend roles within a theme setting and interact cooperatively, improvising dialogue and actions. Initially, the themes are familiar ones such as "the home" or "the grocery store," but gradually more complex settings such as "the post office" or "the airport" are introduced. The children substitute make-believe movements or verbal statements and descriptions for real objects, actions, and situations: "Let's pretend I'm the daddy and this is our lawn mower and I'm cutting the grass."

This type of pretend play is initiated, designed, and controlled by the children who use their imagination to create their own storylines, choose roles, create dialogue, interact, and even monitor what the characters say. To foster dramatic play, the teacher initially provides background information about the theme to prepare the children to play it, and basic props are provided to support the pretense. Otherwise, the role of the teacher is limited to assisting the children to maintain or extend the play as needed through comments or questions or by modeling behavior. Overall, however, the child is the decision maker and in control.

By negotiating plans and clarifying desired behavior, dramatic play provides children with valuable opportunities for language learning (Bodrova and Leong 2003) and is especially significant for children learning English as a second language (Konishi 2007). Sara Smilansky's early and landmark research (1968) provided significant insight concerning the development of dramatic play and introduced the term "sociodramatic play." The two terms "sociodramatic play" and "dramatic play" are frequently used interchangeably today. Smilansky (Smilansky and Shefatya 1990) also emphasized that the dramatization of *provided storylines* was *not* included in her definition of sociodramatic play. Although Smilansky had used story-based drama, she found children reacted differently to the added structure of a provided storyline (Mages 2008). This finding might well reinforce the belief that young children need and benefit from a rich background in improvised dramatic play before engaging in story-based dramatizations, which are more structured by the storyline.

Drama in everyday activities

While the compelling appeal of dramatic play provides a perfect introduction to improvised pretending, as children gain experience, pretending and drama can be gradually woven into other everyday classroom activities. Teachers can introduce a challenging variety of dramatic experiences such as "acting out" sections of picture books or parts of finger plays, nursery rhymes, and poems. These stories can also be altered or completely rewritten and performed with new words and actions and shared with others. All that is needed is a good idea and a lively imagination. This process also enables children to integrate dramatization in other subject areas such as math (performing counting in finger plays), science (miming the development of a flower), or social science (demonstrating the solving of a classroom problem). Games that involve pretending can also be used to extend learning.

Introducing simple mime provides a good starting everyday activity because it enables children to present ideas using wordless gestures and body movements, and is especially helpful to English language learners coping with vocabulary meanings. Paintings and sculpture can also involve pretending by dramatizing the stories portrayed in art, while puppetry enables children to safely convey their thoughts, feelings, and emotions through the words of a puppet. Children can also act out words when singing a song or substitute words and actions when chanting repetitive phrases. They can link a series of body movements or yoga poses when listening to different kinds of melodies. Such dramatic activities can be fairly brief and slipped into the program as learning opportunities arise or when relaxation is needed and appreciated. Everyday pretending can be very flexible.

Story dramatization

As children feel more comfortable pretending, dramatizing an entire story becomes an engaging possibility. This type of pretending differs from dramatic play because children act out well-known storylines rather than create their own. Story dramatization is more sequential and less improvised than dramatic play and more of an overall group effort. Emphasis is placed on interaction, cooperation, and teamwork as children become involved in choosing roles and assignments and planning simple staging, props and costumes. Story dramatization can be especially appealing to reluctant speakers, children with special needs, and English language learners because it enables them to become increasingly involved as they feel comfortable. Initially,

they can choose a non-speaking role or supportive task to perform and still enjoy being involved with their peers in the undertaking.

While story dramatization may sound like "performing a play," the method in this work uses a far more relaxed approach. To begin, a story is impressively *told* by the teacher so that the children can mentally visualize the setting, characters, and events in their minds. Next, a picture-book version of the story is *read* by the teacher and discussed. Then the teacher and the children *together picture-read* the storybook, reviewing the story sequence. By having several different retellings, the children learn the story and can imagine possible ways of dramatizing it. With teacher guidance, they participate in planning and *presenting* the story but in a highly informal manner. The scenery, props, and costumes are usually minimal, with the children using their imagination to create the story atmosphere.

Initially, the teacher narrates the story and the children generally follow the storybook dialogue in portraying the characters. Gradually, however, the teacher begins to simplify the narration by including only basic information and using prompting comments or questions to encourage the children to portray characters with their own words and actions. Often, teacher comments will highlight needed information or details, and the children will follow the clues and begin improvising. Usually, the storyline is generally followed but it can become quite innovative as the children gain experience. Older children often enjoy creating dialogues that take the story in exciting directions. Meanwhile, members of the audience are actively involved in observing, knowing that a lively feedback discussion will follow and that they will be assuming the roles later in a repeat dramatization. Overall, the focus of story dramatization is to provide thinking opportunities rather than a polished performance.

Most groups are satisfied with practicing the story several times and then having an ending performance (or two) for themselves. Older children, however, might decide to plan an informal performance for invited guests such as parents, the cafeteria or office staff, or even going "on the road" to another classroom. Even such a performance does *not* resemble "formal theatre," and this difference needs to be clearly recognized. The emphasis of story dramatization is *not* communicating with an audience or how well the story is performed but rather, what the children have learned from the experience of planning and performing the story. Emphasis is on the *experience of the children* and the warm glow of self-confidence attained through trying and accomplishing.

Sound exciting? It is! An evolving program consisting of dramatic play, integrating pretending and drama in everyday activities, and story dramatization is engaging, challenging, and enjoyable for young children. It stimulates creativity, intellectual growth, and the development of social competence, while practicing skills needed for later school success.

HOW DO STORY PRETENDING AND DRAMA SUPPORT DEVELOPMENT?

Young children tend to be natural dramatists, and the prospect of pretending a story captures their attention and motivates involvement. Pretending stories infuses the classroom with energy and fosters enthusiasm for learning because children are no longer outside the events of a story but actively engaged in it. They *become* the story. In addition to its obvious appeal, there are a variety of ways, both general and specific, in which story pretending is relative to development and learning.

Woodard (1987) described Piaget's view of young children's learning as a process of interacting with people, things, and events, and, through reasoning, building an understanding of their world. Story pretending and drama provide countless opportunities for children to construct knowledge through integrated hands-on experiences, probing discussions, and adult and peer teaching. Piaget's groundbreaking work (1962) emphasized the relationship between play and cognitive development and the importance of representational or symbolic thinking in which children pretend that materials are something they are not. A young child using play dough may announce, "Look, I made a birthday cake," indicating the ability to separate the *idea* of a birthday cake from a *real* birthday cake. Piaget considers this the beginning of true play. As representational thinking develops, children continue to substitute words for actions and objects and consciously use dramatic play in pretend themes creating their own simple storylines. "Let's pretend we went to the park but it rained and now we're home." The players can pretend the story because they agree to use spoken words to represent the events that didn't occur. Gradually, they will realize that spoken words can be written by using letters that represent sounds.

Vygotsky (1967, 1978) not only emphasized the central role of play in cognition but identified the use of language and children's social experiences as fundamental forces in learning. He designated a zone of proximal development in which a child is unable to manage certain tasks alone, but with the support of competent adults or more knowing peers can be successful. Increasing current research suggests that pretending does not emerge spontaneously but rather is the result of social collaboration. Story pretending in which children with different competencies engage in cooperative dialogues and joint problem solving provides scaffolding which enables them to extend the play and foster cognitive growth (Forman 1987). In pretending, language is exchanged and internalized, and the children organize their play efforts accordingly. In this way, story pretending provides a supportive learning environment for those of diverse cultural backgrounds

(Latino/Hispanic, African American, Native American, Asian/Asian American, and European American) who initially become involved by listening and observing the action. Schomburg (1996), however, cautions that children need sufficient time for pretending in order to expand their representational skills and be prepared to manage signs and symbols in later academic assignments. Parents also need to know the importance of pretend play for future learning and be encouraged to support it at home.

Story pretending and drama offer an array of overall benefits that are certainly impressive. Consider some of the possible skills young children can develop:

- representational (symbolic) thinking

- inventive thinking

- mentally visualizing events and ideas

- sequencing events and ideas

- connecting cause and effect and making predictions

- problem solving and decision making

- scaffolding with knowledgeable adults and peers

- transforming creative ideas into action

- extending attention span and memory capacity

- interacting socially and building self-esteem

- communicating through words, gestures, and movement

- planning and collaborating with others

- utilizing feedback from others

- reacting spontaneously to novel behavior of others

- understanding social conventions

- practicing self-discipline and delaying gratification

- respecting the views of others

- extending empathy towards others

- comprehending moral values

- understanding of self and recognizing personal competencies.

In addition, dramatic experiences enable the young child to extend the literacy skills of listening, oral language, writing, and reading into real-world practice. A more comprehensive understanding of these competencies emerges as the specific areas of cognitive development, social/emotional development, and literacy are considered in depth.

Cognitive development

Both dramatization and reading are thinking processes and tend to share similar mental requirements. The ability to represent thought with action and objects (representational thinking) is necessary in pretending a story as well as in reading, in which letters represent sounds that have meaning when combined.

Story pretending enables children to learn about people and events with whom they are unable to have direct experience, and to build essential background knowledge to support emergent reading skills. It also provides opportunities to explore higher-level thinking skills such as analysis, synthesis, and evaluation (Yau 1992). Analysis enables children to break material into understandable parts—for example, the beginning, middle, end of a story—while synthesis is used to reorganize the parts in different ways—for example,

changing the events or dialogue—and evaluation involves judging the value of material. As children use these skills in discussions and exchange feedback, they move from simple facts to explanations (Beals, DeTemple, and Dickinson 1994) and ask questions, reason, associate cause and effect, clarify meanings, and make predictions. Roskos, Christie, and Richgels (2003) note that during dramatic play children stay on task for longer periods of time and may function at higher cognitive levels.

In dramatic play improvised around a theme such as the bakery, there are mutually agreed-upon social rules or ways of enacting the theme. Players will quickly correct each other regarding these understandings. "A baker doesn't sell vegetables!" Children must concentrate and remember to stay within the rules in order to maintain their role and extend the play. This requires self-restraint and a basic understanding of social norms and the behavior needed to support them. Berk (1994) emphasizes the importance Vygotsky placed on rule-based play in developing reflective thinking and self-regulated and cooperative behavior.

As dramatic play involves imitating the talk and behavior of others, memory is utilized in recalling people, actions, and events relative to the event. Performers must be keen observers and alert to the *clues* in the environment, such as a body gesture or a questioning voice, and be flexible in responding and "thinking on their feet" as circumstances change. Players also need to recognize that co-players have their own ideas which need to be discussed, negotiated, and mutually resolved to keep the play moving forward. In this way, children teach and learn from each other.

In dramatizing a specific story, thinking is involved as children struggle to develop the core traits and behaviors of characters and use reasoning to create a believable interpretation of a role. They begin to identify with the character and think about the possible problems, conflicts, dialogues, and negotiations involved, and are able to try to evaluate different presentations of the character. Decisions are made as they imagine and evaluate possible ways to alter the character, setting, and action to improve their portrayal. Comparing their portrayal against a conceptualized "template" of the character builds self-reflection skills as well as a keener understanding of social roles.

Thinking of positive ways to solve problems requires recognizing that different solutions have different consequences for human relationships and life. Young children have limited opportunities for decision making, and entering an imaginary story provides a safe setting to test their ideas without failure or reprisal. Imagination enables the child to suppose, take a guess, or plan, even without sufficient information, to explore reality and determine what is real and what is pretend. Narrative learning creates a connection between imaginary and real environments and supports a new type of problem solving that involves children determining if imaginary solutions can be used in real-world situations with limitations (Hakkarainen 2002).

Story reenactments enabled kindergartners and first graders to have better comprehension and recall of stories than another group who were exposed to art activities and discussion led by a teacher (Pellegrini and Galda 1982). This effect on comprehension might be attributed to the extensive use in drama of imagination and reflection which expands mental imaging and creates a *picture* in one's mind. It also serves to augment creativity (Yau 1992). Young children are seldom able to reflect and rehearse their actions but can do so in drama as they plan and evaluate their roles. An additional advantage is that children can monitor their own comprehension by thinking about misconceptions, overlooked points, and hidden meanings indicated by a character. With this deeper understanding, children can correct inaccuracies and avoid them in the future.

Story dramatization also supports many of the cognitive skills needed for school success. Podlozny (2000) reports that, overall, research indicates that classroom drama helps children understand and recall a story and promotes oral language development. Dramatization also requires sequencing story events and connecting and integrating them appropriately. It is necessary to stretch the attention span and use persistence in enacting a role convincingly while making decisions about voice, words, and gestures. Self-discipline and control develop as children learn to abide by the rules established by the group in a dramatic play undertaking. New avenues of understanding are achieved through such skills as classification, comparing/contrasting, relating cause and effect, comprehension, decision making, and summarization.

Story pretending is also interesting with regards to Gardner's (1983) theory of multiple intelligences. It maintains there is not one single type of intelligence but "many ways of knowing" which are biologically based but environmentally nurtured. A typical classroom tends to emphasize and value linguistic intelligence, which is the ability to communicate, and logical/mathematical intelligence, which makes use of the scientific process. Dramatization, however, fosters other intelligences as well. Staging requires spatial intelligence; interpreting body movement uses body/kinesthetic intelligence; chanting, singing, and movement involve musical/rhythmic intelligence; and naturalistic intelligence is valuable when portraying animals, birds, and elements in nature. The ability to be self-reflective and interact effectively with others also utilizes interpersonal and intrapersonal intelligence. As children have opportunities to rotate dramatic roles and tasks, they can explore a variety of different areas of intelligence and enhance new areas of thinking.

Social/emotional development

Dramatic play, creative drama activities, and story dramatization are cooperative endeavors in which children work together as partners in an adventure, utilizing collaboration to reach a common goal. They become a team, a community of learners who, with adult guidance, exchange ideas, take turns using words to negotiate and solve problems, and learn to extend respect and tolerance to each other. Young children at different levels of competency provide scaffolding for each other as they work in pairs or small and large groups and develop a sense of belonging. Friendships are formed by demonstrations of concern, affection, and helpfulness (Avgitidou 2001), and story pretending offers numerous opportunities to practice prosocial behavior. Pretending nurtures self-mastery skills which enable children to feel competent and think "I can do that!"

Young children tend to believe that others think just as they think. Pretending enables them to place themselves in another's shoes, see things from a different perspective, and develop sensitivity towards others. Drama-related interactions cultivate respect for the thoughts, feelings, and intentions of others, as well as respect for their individuality. Such experiences lessen egocentricity and foster social growth. When improvising a dramatic play role, children obtain immediate and useful feedback from peers while exploring how to give and receive suggestions skillfully. This can nurture a deeper interpretation and understanding of human relations and self-awareness regarding *who I am* in relationship to others.

In story dramatization, children identify with a character and can become more empathetic as they think about the character's experiences, feelings, traits, and motivation. Underlying values are perceived through the moral themes presented in traditional tales that enable children to think about aspects of character. They identify helping behaviors and the ethics of a good person, and recognize the skills of leadership and those of an effective follower. Earlier research (Bordan 1970) found that children who were unable to understand the morals of fables read aloud were able to do so after dramatizing the story. Children performing a story have the opportunity to express themselves before a group and develop fluency and persuasiveness along with sclf-confidence. They also learn to "read" the response of an audience and adapt accordingly. They become more willing to take risks with a role and evaluate their results by asking, "How can I do that better?"

Story dramatization also offers many opportunities to find the best way for each child to contribute. Whether participating as a narrator, a performer, prop manager, or member of the audience, each child's contribution is recognized, and acknowledged as important. Ideas are highly valued. Imagination and creativity are recognized and as children see themselves in a successful new light, they can discover hidden talents not previously expressed. In drama, all children have a chance to be stars and feel competent in an atmosphere free from non-threatening comments.

Pretending provides new outlets for expressing children's thoughts and emotions which otherwise might not be available to them. When young children become restless as they sometimes do, dramatization offers emotional relaxation together with physical activity and the chance to practice motor skills. Vygotysky (2004) emphasized the importance of creative expression in the development of imagination and that young children benefit from involvement in a variety of everyday creative experiences. Clearly, pretending supports social and emotional development through related artistic activities such as painting, sculpture, music, and movement. Indeed, improvised drama is creativity in action!

The literacy connection

Literacy development consists of four distinct but interrelated components—listening, speaking, reading, and writing—and begins long before children start school. It develops while oral language is being acquired as children interact with others in the daily activities of living. As both drama and literacy focus on communication, drama provides numerous opportunities to practice and develop literacy skills.

Hoffman (2010) reviews the difference between two types of literacy skills described by Paris (2005). *Constrained skills*, such as knowledge of the alphabet, awareness of print, and phonological awareness, are explicit skills often taught more directly, are easier to teach and assess, and develop within a fairly brief period of time. *Unconstrained skills*, such as vocabulary, listening, comprehension, critical thinking, and problem solving, are more complex skills which continue to develop through one's lifetime. These are involved in real-life language interactions with teachers and knowledgeable others and are more difficult to acquire and evaluate. Skillful planning is needed to maintain an instructional *balance* between these two types of literacy skills, "so that language and literacy become authentically embedded not only as something to be learned, but also as a way to interact, make meaning, and learn" (Hoffman 2010, p.15). Involvement in dramatic play, integrating drama in everyday activities, and story dramatization help young children construct a balanced foundation of essential language and literacy skills, and the role of the teacher is to engage them meaningfully in such activities. Literacy requires not only adult intervention but the availability of practice and supportive materials.

LISTENING

When listening to stories being read, children begin to understand the *language of literature* and to realize that the words they are hearing come from the print.

Gradually, children learn that written words are made with letters that represent sounds and that letters can be used over and over in different ways to form new words. This process of *understanding the system* forms a language base and is a precursor to reading. Research consistently indicates that the more children know about language and literacy before beginning formal schooling, the more likely they are to succeed in academic ventures (Burns, Griffin, and Snow 1999).

By listening to stories and what others have to say about them, children develop a *listening* vocabulary which aids them in constructing the meaning of words and comprehension. Children hear questions, comments, and explanations when engaged in dramatic activities. They listen to dialogue and when receiving suggestions concerning the playing of a role. In a drama-friendly classroom, good listening skills are practiced continually and attention is focused on sounds, words, syllables, and sentences, as well as ideas and meanings.

SPEAKING

Oral language, writing, and reading are closely interrelated and develop concurrently rather than sequentially. As children in our diverse society interact with others, their language reflects the speech of the family and community. Even if English is the first language, the child's vocabulary, pronunciation, and sentence structure may not be Standard English. There are broad individual differences in language, and young children need many opportunities to discuss their experiences with peers and adults in order to develop language competency. Story pretending and drama is an engaging way to practice and extend speaking skills and, as such, is especially useful to English language learners, children from different cultural backgrounds, and even shy, hesitant speakers.

To foster oral language with less frequent speakers, partner or small group interactions can be highly effective. In the action research of the *Let's Talk* program (Woodard *et al.* 2004), teachers paired a congenial fluent speaker with a less fluent speaker and scheduled the pairs to play and talk together undisturbed for a 15-minute period each day using miniature toys. These included a combination of miniature people figures, house furniture, trucks, farm animals, and wild animals, items usually available in an early childhood classroom. The teacher gradually introduced and modeled using the toys, which were also available to the other children during the week. An evaluation of the program, using a survey reflecting New York State Standards across information, comprehension, vocabulary, main ideas, and gesture factors, showed statistically significant improvement over pre-test scores in these areas for both pre-kindergartners and kindergartners. Teachers reported growth in sentence length and structure, sense of story, and sharing ideas through drawing and writing. They also reported social and emotional growth by the infrequent speakers as bonds were often formed with their partners that extended to other areas and activities. The *Let's Talk* program is aimed directly at extending peer verbalization and can easily be adapted for a variety of early childhood settings.

In story pretending, children learn about eye contact, voice projection and manipulation, and the back-and-forth rhythm of talking, and they explore facial expressions, body language, and vocabulary. The teacher's modeling of speech in group discussions provides guidance for children in planning dramatic play themes or discussing and evaluating informal story dramatizations. Through such exchanges, children begin to unlock a more sophisticated level of story comprehension. Children are also quick to recognize the importance of the spoken word as they realize its usefulness in capturing and holding the interest of their peers.

WRITING

Long before children master the skill of writing, they have observed adults writing in a variety of ways, such as making grocery lists or writing telephone messages. They understand that writing is important and often pretend to write for real purposes during dramatic play. Initially, children express their thoughts through drawing or picture writing which gradually develops to include scribbles to represent words. Eventually, strings of letters replace the scribbles and some sounds are matched to letters. As children gain confidence, words begin to have initial and ending sounds, and some vowels may be inserted, though often incorrectly. However, the ability to write words the way they sound is a major step forward. Writing is an involved process and requires much practice which can be obtained by weaving writing into dramatic activities. Children can practice by drawing, dictating, or writing about a dramatic play theme, a puppet activity, or an individual story they have composed. Items such as labels, signs, charts, tickets, invitations, and thank-you notes can also be written. These writing activities involve real-life needs and reflect the value of writing in *getting things done*. When writing practice is built into children's activities, it makes sense and can be undertaken at the individual child's level of development. In an environment where meaningful writing occurs, young children become able writers.

READING

Learning to read is an abstract task that involves identifying and manipulating the individual sounds in words. By "playing" with language, children develop such skills as recognizing specific sounds in a word and identifying the different sounds in a set of words. Other concepts include blending and separating sounds to make a word and adding, omitting, and substituting sounds to create a new word. Such skills are essential for children to understand that letters represent spoken sounds and how these sounds work together. Children learn to manipulate sounds through a variety of experiences. Perlmutter, Folger, and Holt (2009) relate how pre-kindergarten children were introduced to most of the letters and sounds of the alphabet by "reading" laminated cards at roll call printed with each child's name. Such techniques can be easily adapted and used in dramatic activities.

Through dramatization, young children also gain a strong sense of how a story is structured (McMaster 1998). They begin to understand that a story has a beginning, middle, and an end, along with sequenced events and generally a problem and a solution. Children realize that a story has a setting—where it takes place and a time frame such as long ago, today, or in the future—and a cast of characters. Gradually, they build an understanding of word order, phrasing, and punctuation, and grasp the difference between fantasy and reality. Dramatization also promotes vocabulary and comprehension which are fundamental components of reading. New vocabulary used within the context of dramatic activities involves the whole child in constructing the meaning of words. As the main purpose of reading is to understand what has been read, the National Reading Panel (2000) underscores the importance of scaffolding, questioning and discussing, modeling the thinking process, and engaged active involvement as necessary to the development of comprehension. Drama involves such strategies which stimulate children's capacity to analyze material.

It is also essential to share information about literacy development with parents along with suggestions as to how to foster it in the home setting. Parents need to know that literacy and knowledge go hand in hand (Neuman and Dickinson 2001), and practicing listening, speaking, writing, and reading cultivates thinking skills required for future success in school. To assist busy parents, Appendix A "Home-Based Literacy Activities", contains a variety of activities that can be included in parent communications.

WHY ARE STORY PRETENDING AND DRAMA NEGLECTED IN THE CLASSROOM?

With such an extensive list of benefits, story pretending seems a natural addition to early childhood classrooms, but often it is not included for various reasons. One reason is that the ability to *tell* a good story seems to be a fast-fading art. Teachers trained in the early 20th century mastered the skill of storytelling and had a repertoire of told stories that helped children to form story pictures in their minds (Muegel, private taped interview). With the increased publication of children's books and the advent of television and the computer, visual images have gradually replaced mental ones and imagination is less utilized.

Struggling to cover a multitude of topics, today's teacher training programs often assign minimal preparation time to story pretending and drama. Ways of including or integrating it may be limited or not covered. Consequently, teachers may well feel unprepared to facilitate dramatic activities (Furman 2000). Lacking background, teachers may not fully appreciate the value of dramatization and may even question its inclusion, especially in a structured academic schedule. Certainly, they might feel inadequate when attempting to explain its value to questioning administrators, board members, or curious parents.

Teachers may also think of story dramatization as an elaborate scripted "play" which could seem overwhelming and a time-consuming burden. As in art, there is the temptation to focus on the final *product*—a performance—instead of the *experiences* that develop children's competencies. As story dramatization involves the entire class, teachers may hesitate, fearing that drama's playfulness might encourage children to take learning less seriously and relax self-control.

Probably the major reason, however, why drama is now underutilized is the present educational climate. In the current effort to raise academic achievement, scripted materials focusing on isolated skills, teacher-directed instruction, rote learning, and increased preparation for standardized testing are often imposed on teachers and young children, limiting the time allotted to creative activities. As a consequence, recent research indicates a steady fall of scores on the Torrence Tests of Creative Thinking from 1990 to 2008. Moyer further describes the current curriculum changes as being brought about by "societal pressure, misunderstandings about how children learn, aggressive marketing of commercial materials largely inappropriate for kindergarten-age children, a shortage of teachers specifically prepared to work with young children, and the reassignment of trained teachers in areas of declining enrollment" (2001, p.l6l). Schools also face excessive financial constraints and continued pressure to limit or even eliminate the arts. In addition, sedentary technical devices such as television, computer games, cell phones, and texting promote solitary play and limit the development of interpersonal skills.

It is precisely when teachers feel pressured to use structured, "one type fits all" instruction that story pretending and drama need to be tucked into the planning book in order to promote children's joy of learning. Reservations about how to accomplish this fade quickly as teachers consider innovative ways to provide dramatic experiences. Experience indicates the most effective strategy is to begin simply…and have a plan!

HOW CAN THIS BOOK HELP?

The remainder of this book provides a comprehensive guide for teachers interested in beginning to use story pretending and drama as well as those searching for new and novel approaches.

Chapter 2, "Setting the Stage for Story Pretending and Drama", centers on creating a drama-friendly class environment that invites and extends the use of pretending. It contains suggestions for arranging the room with story pretending and drama in mind, and includes materials for areas such as blocks, art, and music, and the class library. As dramatization requires mutual trust and teamwork to support risk taking, ideas for creating a caring classroom are also covered. The teacher guides the children in developing respectful listening and speaking skills through discussion, skillful questioning, and active modeling. The importance of parent involvement is stressed, and numerous ways are offered to draw parents into children's dramatic undertakings.

Part 2, "Including Story Pretending and Drama in the Classroom: Lights, Camera, Action!", sequentially discusses the three types of drama highlighted in the book, beginning with dramatic play using themes, followed by integrating drama in everyday story, art, and music activities, and concluding with preparations to present a story dramatization.

Chapter 3, "Lights: Beginning with Dramatic Play," covers the introduction of dramatic play and the importance of background information in planning a play theme such as the bakery store. A variety of play theme settings, ranging from simple to complex, are described and include basic materials to facilitate the play. The role of the teacher in guiding dramatic play and suggestions for observing, recording, and assessing drama play skills are also presented.

Chapter 4, "Camera: Adding Story Pretending and Drama to Everyday Activities," provides a variety of workable ways to integrate drama into everyday activities, including stories and drama (mime, finger plays, nursery rhymes and poems, and picture books), art and drama (pictures and artists, sculpture, and puppetry), and music and drama (songs and instruments, movement and yoga).

Chapter 5, "Action: Getting Ready for Story Dramatization," introduces the process of preparing

children to dramatize a story by first learning it and then participating in its planning. To learn a story well enough to dramatize involves encountering it in different ways. To accomplish this, the teacher first *tells* the story, then *reads* the storybook aloud, and finally, *picture-reads* the storybook *with* the children. The children are included in overall planning from assigning roles and tasks to designing simple staging, props, and costumes. Ideas regarding practices, informal performances, and observing and assessing drama skills are also suggested. This preparatory section paves the way for an informal story dramatization actually to happen.

Part 3, "The Performance: Curtain Going Up!," is unique in that it provides a comprehensive guide to informally dramatizing a specific story, *The Three Billy Goats Gruff.* A main feature is the inclusion of a picture-book version of this nursery tale with striking, colorful, hand-cut silhouette illustrations. These are especially effective for beginning picture reading, and optional teacher's prompting questions are included. This "book within a book" can be used in different ways to facilitate learning the story. It can guide teachers in preparing to tell the story, be read aloud to the children, and then picture-read by the teacher and the children together. Another benefit of the book is that additional copies can be downloaded from www.jkp.com and printed for classroom and home use.

Hands-on activities to use or adapt in planning the dramatization are also included. These include suggestions for simple scenery, props, and costumes, as well as ways to integrate literacy and other related areas. A practice walk-through of the dramatization illustrates the process of using teacher-prompting comments to encourage children to improvise and use their own words and actions. This section enables teachers to help young children plan and present a beginning story drama with ease, and builds a solid foundation for dramatizing other favorite stories in the future.

At some point, the question may arise: What about reading different storybook versions to the children? By all means, when an appropriate version is available, use it and talk about the similarities and differences involved.

There is no "one way" to use story pretending and drama with young children. The approach presented in this book is designed to provide stimulating, interactive ways for teachers and children to get started

in dramatization. As an all-inclusive resource, this book offers valuable assistance for busy teachers and parents to understand story pretending and drama and use it to facilitate learning. Teachers are encouraged to expand this initial introduction by using their own creative ideas and to move above and beyond the suggestions in the book. In summary, this book provides teachers with a comprehensive resource offering enough guidance to feel comfortable in implementing story pretending and drama and enough decision-making opportunities to feel creative in the process.

Chapter 2

SETTING THE STAGE FOR STORY PRETENDING AND DRAMA

THE ROOM

Creativity blossoms in a creative work space, so it is important to begin with the room arrangement. First, consider basic room guidelines such as being able to view the entire room at once, establishing good traffic routes, and limiting the amount of furniture and materials. Then, keeping dramatization in mind, evaluate the space available. Try to assign a large space to language arts, by combining the reading, writing, talking, and listening areas or keeping them near one another. During the early part of the year, these areas can be used for specific literacy activities, but, later, certain areas can be temporarily used for planning, practicing, and performing informal story dramatizations. Using the reading/library area for performing is a logical approach as both share similar needs. Each requires an open area away from distractions, good lighting, and enough space to allow about three inches (8 cm) between children when whole group seating is needed. Comfortable seating can include moveable carpet squares, chair seat pads, or even travel-size pillows. A small beanbag chair can invite a three-year-old to read to a stuffed toy, while a basket of puppets can stimulate pretend conversations between friends.

To encourage picture reading among younger children and English language learners, use room signs to label areas and materials, and place pictures before the identifying words. Pictures can be simple line drawings or cut from supply catalogues. Provide a flannelboard (Chapter 5) with several sets of pictures of figures copied from familiar storybooks (Chapter 4), which children can use to tell stories to each other. Talk about "reading" pictures to obtain information and to encourage them to think of themselves as readers. For more picture-reading practice, place a rectangular box in the library area filled with predictable books that have easy-to-follow pictures to accompany the texts. Add some puppets to the library area where they can be used to do picture reading. For English language learners, *beginning* picture books of familiar objects with identifying words below can be used with a helpful friend, or ask a parent to take photographs of frequently used classroom items, add lower-case identifying words, and insert them in an album for viewing.

Include books reflecting the cultural backgrounds of the children in the group. Provide books at different reading levels and suggest the children explore the books and select one to read or picture-read individually or with a friend. This approach enables children to enjoy picture reading even if they choose a book with a more challenging text. To encourage conversation, place interesting pictures at the children's eye level and talk about them at story time. Some large magazine advertisements can be intriguing and also very humorous. Change the pictures periodically to maintain and stimulate interest and discussion. Talking sets the stage for drama by giving hesitant speakers or those with limited verbal skills the chance to begin sharing ideas and feeling more comfortable participating. Simple room details can support the development of both story pretending and literacy.

Drama is based on a love of stories, so library books are a major consideration in room planning. Display the front covers (not just the spines) of a few captivating books along with others on the shelves. Avoid having too many books available at one time as it can be distracting and complicate decision making. Instead, rotate or change some of the books on a regular basis, perhaps every two or three weeks, to keep the supply fresh and inviting. Of course, certain old favorites should always remain available. A parent could assume this changing assignment.

Children enjoy many kinds of books, so a wide variety is needed: picture books, wordless books, number and alphabet books, and informational books about animals, plants, people, machines, and other themes of interest. Include also bilingual dictionaries and a variety of books representing the children's cultural backgrounds. Nonfiction books are favorites among young children and add to their knowledge base and foster reflective thinking. Picture dictionaries help expand vocabulary and provide information through picture reading. Nursery rhymes, poetry books, and those focusing on sounds, rhyming, and alliteration need to be included, together with books dealing with character development. Predictable stories and fables are particularly suitable for dramatization, so this supply should be highlighted. During the early part of the year, children can become familiar with the storylines of a number of fables. Then, later, after they have performed *The Three Billy Goats Gruff*, they can revisit these well-known stories and choose others to dramatize. A list of favorite books to dramatize is provided on p.76.

Look for other novel ways to promote pretending and drama in the classroom. In the writing area, add unusual ink pad stamps such as those with the name of the day and alphabet letters, colored stamp pads, and homemade picture/word (p.131) cards to provide a resource when drawing or writing about a favorite story. Place laminated strips (3 × 12 inches/8 × 30 cm) around the room containing the lower- and upper-case alphabet to use as a ready reference, rather than having to refer to a distant wall chart. Add a class list with photographs and names so the children can picture-read faces and write messages to each other. Again, seek out a helping parent for this task.

Talk about mailing a letter and make a simple mailbox for sending and receiving class mail. Provide writing supplies around the room rather than just at the writing table. Pencils, pads, and large sheets of paper are needed to write notes, letters, labels, signs, and turn sheets. Providing a wide array of art materials, such as various sizes and colors of paper, pencils, crayons, magic markers, and poster paint, enables children to imagine and create a story picture, and the teacher can offer to write the story below using the children's own words.

Typing paper can also be folded into a four-page booklet for writing stories. Some children enjoy adding a touch of humor while composing by wearing headbands announcing "The author is writing!"

To conserve space in the listening area, equipment can be stored in a large plastic tub. This tub becomes a listening center when emptied and turned upside down on the floor with the listening equipment placed on top. Children need to be taught how to use the equipment, so place a large picture/word chart of the steps involved posted at eye level by the tub. They can also pretend while listening and moving to all kinds of music from classical to jazz, or hearing recorded indoor and outdoor sounds on CDs. Talk about the sounds "I think I hear thunder or is that a train going by? What do you think? What do you hear now?" Listening to commercial CDs of various nature or animal sounds or taping the children's sound effects encourages them to listen, recognize, and imitate sounds.

For three- and four-year-olds, a block area in the room provides strong support for make-believe and speech production. People figures, miniature furniture, and domestic and wild animal figures should be included in the block area to enhance pretending, along with items that can be used to represent other things, such as a paper cup turned upside down to become a pretend hill. Children can build the setting for a favorite story on the floor or a tabletop and use it to retell the story to a friend or the class.

Posting pictures of different kinds of constructions, and labeled "house," "skyscraper," "bridge," encourages picture reading and designing. Include, too, pictures of famous buildings such as the Guggenheim Museum, the Lincoln Memorial, or a photograph of a familiar building in the community. Provide picture/word signs such as "hospital," "police," or the logo sign for McDonald's famous arches. Pretending and planning can be stimulated by requesting children to include specific features in their building—for example, four windows, two doors, and a stairway to the attic. Then the children can pretend a story about the building and tell it to the group. If the project requires several days, the builders can add a sign: "Please do not touch."

There are sound reasons why the dramatic play area deserves special attention in room planning as this popular area offers unlimited opportunities to make-believe. Early in the school year, three- and four-year-olds enjoy a house setting, including a table, chairs, dishes, a pretend stove, and dolls representing major ethnic groups. This setting invites pretending because the children are familiar with these things from their own homes. Older kindergartners and first graders might prefer a dramatic play area with a full-length unbreakable mirror and a collection of simple story-related props and costumes to explore. The children can also compile a wish list of interesting dress-up items such as a football jersey, an Indian sari, or a Mexican sombrero; parents are usually happy to share some of their more exotic attire. It is often surprising what forgotten treasures become available and stimulate story pretending and drama. Later, the dramatic play area can be related to a community theme that the children are studying and become an operating bank with tellers, play money, deposit slips, and check books. By arranging the space and adding different props for different themes, the dramatic play area can be transformed into a variety of settings that provide valuable practice in story pretending and drama.

Younger children and those with less make-believe experience tend to need more realistic props in dramatic play than older children, but most props can be homemade as long as they are fairly realistic, easy to use, durable, and safe. As with books, too many props can be distracting. Removing those that are less used and adding a few new props from time to time tends to keep children interested and involved.

DEVELOPING A DRAMA-FRIENDLY ENVIRONMENT

Oral language not only helps build the foundation for early literacy, but it is a central element in dramatization. Young children need many opportunities to use and practice this valuable tool with others because it is through speech that dramatic skills and literacy are developed at a time when reading skills are still limited.

The high diversity of today's schools underscores the need for a supportive environment for English language learners who can find the classroom a confusing and risky place. Classroom displays can include posters, typical clothing, and other cultural items that represent the students' diversity and convey that their backgrounds are important. Children with emerging second language skills can be silent at first and only gradually move from one or two words to phrases and sentences. Briefly worded efforts to communicate need to be accepted with respect and focus on the idea the child is trying to express rather than the grammatical form. Teachers can model by speaking more slowly and clearly, using common words, and pausing at natural intervals. The use of repetition and imitation within a drama activity, along with pictures and other visuals that signify an activity, assist children coping with limited verbal skills, language delays, or disabilities. If confusion is evident ask, "Do you understand? Should I say it again?" Body language and gestures, facial expressions, agreed-upon sign language, and acting out words can further aid understanding. In turn, children can use these techniques to respond together with a picture or other visual aids to illustrate their thinking.

Talking with children

Teaching involves intentionally engaging students in language, which enables them to gain knowledge of the real world around them. Often, however, speech is not an exchange of ideas but composed mainly of comments by the teacher. Research indicates that when preschool children are engaged in conversations, the major part of the time is spent talking or listening to the teacher (Dickinson and Sprague 2002). Current programs utilizing teacher-directed instruction or scripted responses are limiting and often tightly scheduled, making it difficult for teachers to find time for natural conversations. One way to solve this challenge is to insert brief talking times throughout the day, integrating them in the daily classroom experiences. Try also to arrange moments when you can talk with children individually. These may initially consist of two or three exchanges and gradually be expanded.

An effective way to encourage talking is to include skillful questions that children find challenging and want to answer. Topics can vary from solving a class problem to determining how to make a prop for a story dramatization. A circle seating arrangement works well for group discussions as the children can see each other and gauge reactions. Try moving around the circle for responses, with the option that it is all right to pass and not respond at all. Use open-ended teacher questions because these questions have many possible replies which encourage children to use words in sharing and reasoning. Open-ended questions that begin with "how," "what," "when," "where," "why," and "which" tend to generate a lot of thinking responses. For example, "How did you feel about the way the story ended?" In contrast, closed questions are more limiting because they can be answered by "Yes" or "No" or very few words and usually have a right or wrong answer. If you ask, "What color is the pumpkin?" you will probably receive a one word answer: "Orange," whereas asking, "What can you tell us about the pumpkin?" stimulates ideas. Early in the year, begin with questions that relate to the children's experiences: "What do you like to eat for breakfast? What fun things do you like to do with your family?" Later, include questions about the story they are planning to dramatize: "What part of *The Three Billy Goats Gruff* story did you like best? Why would you

like to meet the troll?" If a child's response is unclear, rephrase the question to help clarify her/his thinking. Encourage talking by encouraging elaboration: "What do you mean by that? Can you tell us more? Why do you think so?" To expand reasoning, seek support from the group: "Can anyone add anything to Mackenzie's idea? Can anyone share a different idea?"

The teacher can also model phrases that support talking: "That's a really interesting thing to know. I like the way you told us about that." Allow enough time— at least three seconds—for children to process their thoughts before they respond. At times, it is helpful to say, "Wait. Close your eyes and just think about your answer." The teacher can even model the use of thinking time: "Let me think about that question. (Pause) Hmm… Well, maybe…" When searching for ideas, recognize and accept all responses equally. Overenthusiasm for one response can indicate that ideas are being judged, and children may feel reluctant to take that risk and become involved. Even if an idea is unlikely, it doesn't matter because the object is to talk about possibilities. Responses such as "Really?," "You think so?" or "That's possible" convey that everyone's ideas are accepted and respected. Even so, questioning can be overused, so be ready to move on when interest wanes.

Reading and discussing stories provides yet another opportunity to help young children feel comfortable in sharing thoughts. Current research emphasizes that when talking about stories, the main ideas of the story should be discussed to provide additional insight concerning the content (McKeown and Beck 2006). Teachers can plan meaningful comments and questions to help children explain, elaborate, and connect the story ideas. When children have difficulty in responding, the related section of the text should be reread and discussed for clarification, rather than have the teacher provide the needed information. Teachers also need to listen closely to the children's responses in order to understand their thinking and provide effective scaffolding.

Establishing classroom guidelines

Story pretending and drama flourishes in an atmosphere that is both organized and predictable and viewed by children as safe and inviting. A starting goal is to establish a caring room environment in which children work together and respect the ideas and well-being of others. To accomplish this, children need to be involved in establishing classroom guidelines and discuss the reasons for them. Involvement is important because children are motivated to follow rules they help create and understand the reasons for their use.

For clarity, rules need to be stated simply and be specific rather than general. A rule such as "Be kind" is not as helpful as discussing "What do we see/hear when someone is kind?" Rules can then be created from the children's responses. Rules that are stated positively tell children what to do rather than what not to do. Remind by saying, "Walk slowly," rather than, "Don't run." This way, children do not have to translate from the negative to the positive to know what behavior is expected. More general rules such as "Share supplies," "Take turns," and "Include others" are especially meaningful when acted out with peers. Role-playing rules familiarize children with problems before they occur and provides an opportunity to practice solving them in advance. Somewhat older children can benefit from discussing what and why certain behaviors are "unfair" and not allowed in the classroom—for example, name calling, teasing, laughing at mistakes. The baseball term "foul ball" can be introduced to their vocabulary and used effectively to label such behaviors.

Children talking together

Children can often benefit by learning *how* to support each other when talking and sharing ideas. A basic introduction can explain that a question *asks* someone something and a comment *tells* someone something, and include practice using both. Guide the children in discussing effective ways of communicating in a group, such as listening to the speaker, taking turns and talking one at a time, and using a voice that everyone can hear. Discuss and practice how they can help the speaker by looking at her/him, smiling, or nodding slightly to show they are listening and that the words being spoken are important.

Think of all the talking opportunities that occur during the school day which can play an important role in developing a supportive environment. A friendly classroom is based on sensitivity to others, and caring and politeness need to be discussed, practiced, and reinforced to become part of the children's behavior: "Thank you." "Pardon me." "Please pass the paste." When the audience provides feedback after a story dramatization, the teacher can model how to offer a pleasant comment *before* giving a suggestion: "I liked how you jumped into the tub. You could lift your feet a little higher when you march." Respectful ways of receiving comments and suggestions can also be identified and practiced: "Thank you for saying that. That was a helpful thing to tell me."

Opportunities can be planned for children to practice speaking before the group. The children can sign up weekly to present an interesting, touchable item brought from home. Items can include photographs or drawings, but toys are *not* allowed. To start, use a simple format for the presenter: "I brought…," "I like it because…" and "Who has a question or comment?" Simple guidelines can be introduced such as: stay on the topic and avoid repeating the same question. This activity can be tucked into a break during the day and responses can be limited by agreement if necessary.

A frequently heard phrase in a caring classroom is "Use your words." Guidance, practice, and gentle but firm reminders are especially important during the early days of school to establish an environment in which story pretending and drama will thrive.

INVOLVING PARENTS IN STORY PRETENDING AND DRAMA

Parents tend to be enthusiastic about young children starting school and are interested in becoming involved in their children's education. It is the perfect time to establish a partnership with parents and to convey how important it is for them to understand the learning process and reinforce needed skills at home. Henderson and Mapp (2002) found that children from all family backgrounds and income levels gained from programs that involve the family.

About the time of World War II, cooperative nursery schools were widely available and gave parents an opportunity to assist the teacher in the classroom on a regular basis and learn firsthand about curriculum and strategies. Teachers were able to share their knowledge and skills with parents who benefitted from this valuable resource. In turn, parents were able to form sharing and supportive relationships with one another. With more mothers entering the workforce and facing time limitations, this type of participation has become less feasible. Nevertheless, parent involvement remains an essential component in teaching young children.

Not only can parents benefit from interacting with an experienced professional, but teachers can gain valuable insight too. When parents and teachers share understandings of a child's development and shape educational goals together, they form a united working team. As today's classroom is very different in terms of language, family structure, and cultural backgrounds and customs, teachers may find it challenging to grasp the degree of diversity involved. Parent participation can illuminate the real environment of the child and provide needed guidance for the teacher. In turn, parents with diverse backgrounds can learn about the school environment and feel more accepted and comfortable in it. Grandparents should also be considered as many share parenting responsibilities or have the time, interest, and energy to make valuable program contributions. Even within a challenging schedule, part of the teacher's role is to help parents understand what, why, and how their children are learning at school and ways they can support the learning. Porche (2001) indicates that many teachers have not been instructed in the compelling importance of the preschool years in literacy development and the role of the parent in fostering it. While focusing on parental understanding requires additional teacher effort, parent involvement provides unlimited benefits.

Communication is the key. Begin right away to reach out and establish a welcoming environment that conveys that parents are an important link in a child's education. Teachers can start by providing a simple pamphlet describing school guidelines *prior* to children starting school. Providing information before an initial parent meeting allows time for parents to organize questions and comments. A brief outline of the developmental characteristics for the age group is also helpful, along with the emphasis that it is only a guide and that all children develop at their own pace. *Yardsticks* by Chip Wood (1997) is a useful resource for providing this type of developmental information. If English language learner parents are in the group, a bilingual parent can provide a translation of the pamphlet and outline. Such materials indicate the importance of home/school

teamwork and provide a useful reference during the school year.

For initial parent gatherings, consider circular seating to create a relaxed atmosphere where ideas can be exchanged. Begin by discussing the school guidelines and move to reviewing the developmental outline. This often places the meeting on a lighthearted note as parents acknowledge some of the charming but challenging characteristics their young children share. As reading is often of interest to parents, this could be an opportune time to mention the importance of literacy development ("The literacy connection," p.24) and that parents can encourage it in the home setting. Advise parents that you will be sending suggestions for literacy activities that the family can enjoy together (see Appendix A, "Home-Based Literacy Activities"). Rather than one large group evening meeting for parents, two smaller groups could be scheduled at different times if this is more convenient for everyone. Over the first few weeks, some teachers like to arrange brief chats with parents focusing on their *primary goal* for their child for the year. Stone and Chakraborty (2011) suggest calling home early in the year and briefly sharing a positive comment concerning the child—what a pleasant introduction to school and effective way to foster parental support.

As children begin to use the dramatic play theme area in the classroom, an outlined news note can share with parents some of the cognitive, social, and emotional benefits of dramatic play and its tie to literacy. They will be interested to know that dramatic play enables children to *represent* things and events and that this valuable skill helps them understand that letters *represent* sounds in words. Other ideas can also be shared with parents by email or by posting an eye-catching notice with photos on the room door, or whatever means proves most effective. If using a written communication, a simple, quick-to-read outline can emphasize the basics. This format ensures that busy parents are not overwhelmed by words or jargon.

To foster parent involvement, compose a parent interest survey which is easy for parents to check or underline. Leave space for parents to describe how they can help and to add their ideas and suggestions. Such a survey might include:

- Do you have a hobby or a special talent to share such as drawing, storytelling, singing, or playing an instrument?

- Can you share cultural traditions and celebrations, native songs, costumes, or family stories and histories?

- Can you do woodworking, sewing, cooking, or practice yoga or a sport with the children?

- Do you have an occupation or business the children would like to learn about and perhaps visit?

- Can you help with indoor or outdoor activities, accompany field trips, repair toys, help make classroom materials, or telephone or send emails about class information?

Once identified, parental interests can be integrated into classroom activities and support and enrich them.

To facilitate parent activities, ask two or three parents who perhaps have flexible schedules to serve as "room guides" (or coaches, or advisors) to help with room planning and details. By using a team approach, tasks can be divided, with less work for each parent, and teams can be changed during the year. These parents can plan casual gatherings to encourage parent/teacher and parent/parent relationships. They might arrange an informal coffee hour after school or at someone's home or a community center during an evening or weekend, much like those used to introduce election candidates. In addition to the above, a "make and take" afternoon or evening might be scheduled to enable parents to meet while constructing simple materials for home or classroom use. Other parents can always help the current room guides. Some photo-conscious parent might plan a display of enlarged dramatic play photos for the school foyer, or another might burn a CD of a classroom story dramatization to send home for viewing.

Planning a story dramatization provides even more opportunities for parent involvement. Think about the beginning play *The Three Billy Goats Gruff* which the children will be dramatizing and ask, "How can parents help?" Then list the tasks so parents know what help is needed and request them to select an option or two. Try to offer different ways and times that will appeal to parents' talents, interests, and schedules. Emphasize that all involvement, large or small, is appreciated and conveys to children that what they are doing is important.

The following suggestions enable parents to be part of *The Three Billy Goats Gruff* dramatization:

- Provide inexpensive materials needed to dramatize the story, such as pieces of pretend fur material for goat tails or the cardboard backing from large writing pads to make picture/word signs.

- Collect needed props and costume items which the children have suggested, such as paper flowers, empty eye glasses for the troll, or bells for the goats.

- Help children create simple headbands or picture/word signs.

- Help children make a simple stage background with large boxes.

- Help children make advertising posters or invitations for a performance for others or serve simple refreshments afterwards.

- Use the school copy machine to print several copies of *The Three Billy Goats Gruff* storybook (downloaded from www.jkp.com) to send home on a rotating basis. The children can select a character to dramatize while family members narrate the story and assume other roles. Grandparents are often great actors.

- Attend a performance and bring grandparents and friends.

- Videotape a final performance so copies can be made for take-home viewing.

Part 2

INCLUDING STORY PRETENDING AND DRAMA IN THE CLASSROOM

Lights, Camera, Action!

Chapter 3

LIGHTS: BEGINNING WITH DRAMATIC PLAY

Young children need many opportunities to be involved in dramatic play which they create and control. In dramatic play, children enact the roles of adults in their world by actually portraying them and creating their own storyline and dialogue. Participating in dramatic play enables young children to select their own pretend symbols to represent objects, actions, and events to use in their stories. This differs from the story dramatization of *The Three Billy Goats Gruff* presented in Part 3. This story dramatization, while designed to emphasize imagination and improvisation, uses other people's storyline and symbols and is therefore less spontaneous than dramatic play. The child-directed nature of dramatic play *prepares* children for the storyline involved in story dramatization and is an important precursor to it.

INTRODUCING DRAMATIC PLAY

For many young children, being involved in the fantasy of dramatic play is a big step, so it's wise to begin simply. The house theme, being very familiar to children, is a comfortable place to start. After the children have had sufficient time using this theme, introduce a new theme related to the children's real lives as such themes are the most significant and appealing. The actual timing of themes is the teacher's decision and depends mainly on the children's age, degree of interest, and involvement. Generally, themes are available for two or three weeks, and often several weeks elapse between themes so the children can acquire needed background information and help plan the new theme. Children need to know about a theme in order to play it effectively, and the need for background information and planning involvement can unfortunately be overlooked or not fully valued. They are, however, essential supportive elements in dramatic play.

After selecting a theme, think of the possible learning involved and plan your objectives for the undertaking. Consider, too, what the children need to know about both the theme and the individual roles, as children tend to slip in and out of roles during dramatic play. Each role is governed by "rules of behavior," and in order to keep a role among their peers, children must enact it as convincingly as possible. Even a common theme such as the grocery store can be confusing when the child decides to change from the role of cashier to that of stockperson. To understand what is involved in the roles is primary, and this preparation can be accomplished in a variety of ways. A well-planned field trip provides valuable overall background knowledge. In preparing to play the grocery store, for example, try to locate a nearby store with a child-friendly owner and arrange for the class to visit. Consider inviting a parent or two to accompany small groups within the class. Discuss the visit with the children, including safety aspects. Then discover their interests by asking, "What would you like to know about a grocery store?" Note the children's interests and list the questions they would like answered. For example:

- Where do the vegetables come from?
- How does the food get to the store?
- Who bakes the bread and cookies?
- Who puts the food on the shelves?

Be sure to advise the owner of the children's interests and the information that needs to be simply and briefly presented. If a local field trip is not practical, a classroom visitor can be an effective substitute. In preparation for a veterinarian's office theme, an obliging veterinarian might bring a pet cat to school and conduct a physical examination and answer questions. Reading a carefully selected themed picture book can provide a creditable amount of information which can be extended by discussion. Equally effective theme introductions include viewing and discussing a DVD or parent-made PowerPoint® presentation, posters, pictures, and photographs, a puppet presentation, or inviting a parent to demonstrate a theme-related skill. The aim is to find a way that effectively expands the children's understanding of the theme as this is basic to portraying it spontaneously.

After acquiring the background information, think, talk, and plan with the children about arranging the space, and gathering and making some basic props: "What will we need if we're going to play grocery store?" Perhaps make a list. "What could we use instead of a grocery cart?" Welcome ideas. There is always a temptation for the teacher to assume management by arranging the space, providing the materials, and "shaping" the play. While more support may be needed when first introducing dramatic play, overemphasis on direction or academic goals can overwhelm and limit imaginative play. Learning opportunities need to be available but not imposed. Children benefit from exploring their own ideas freely and being actively involved in decision making, beginning with planning the theme.

On the "opening day" of a new theme, review the roles involved and necessary rules such as the number of children allowed to play in the setting and keeping the props in the play area. It is helpful to teach the children to use a "taking turns" chart, especially for a popular theme, so that participation is rotated and everyone has a turn. Then, as the play begins, assume the role of a fairly unobtrusive observer. Regardless of the antics and humor involved, avoid showing amusement and use the time as an opportunity to observe and learn more about the children's behavior. Reflective observation can provide invaluable information about children's play needs and the type of adult intervention needed to foster skills that are lacking.

When observing the play, be alert to confusion or when the play might be faltering by repeating itself again and again or jumping about in a fragmented manner. It is important to know when and when not to intervene and to do so selectively. Helpful questions to consider are: Do the children have good ideas? Do they need more help? If they do need help, now is the time to provide some "outside intervention," not to direct the play but to stimulate fresh thinking. Outside intervention involves using a comment, suggestion, or question to facilitate contact among the players such as "You could both put the food cans on the shelves.

How could you help Taylor find what she wants to buy? Do you need someone to put the food in the bags?" Responsive intervention encourages children to use their own information, experiences, and talents in continuing and enriching the play. If more extensive help is needed, "inside intervention" can be used. This strategy requires joining the play, assuming a role, and modeling appropriate behavior by addressing the character the child is portraying rather than the individual child. Even when inside intervention is necessary, it should not control the content of the play but rather maintain and expand it. Some teachers might hesitate to use intrusive guidance, but children tend to enjoy the attention which can be a catalyst to the play by making them more aware of the possibilities involved. Children learn needed play skills through modeling and demonstrating, and the teacher's skill in scaffolding dramatic play is important to its development.

From time to time in the liveliness of pretending, items in the setting can become disorganized, and it will be necessary to pause and assist the children in rearranging to establish order and make the area playable again. Occasionally, when intervention techniques are not successful and the play becomes inappropriate, it may be necessary to limit the play or even stop it. When this happens, talk about the situation later with the children to determine ways to avoid the problem in the future. Omit individual children's names in the discussion, focusing instead on the problem and possible solutions.

DRAMATIC PLAY THEMES AND MATERIALS

Many young children today spend long hours in writing and reading instruction and very little time in "learning by doing" activities. To help justify dramatic play, especially in a more structured kindergarten or first grade, play themes can be related to a variety of classroom topics being studied. Background information for a medical theme can include science information about body parts and germs or new vocabulary words such as "cavity," "gums," or "hygienist." Themes can also be expanded by introducing creative activities such as related finger plays and songs or writing stories and making books. The themes below are fairly familiar to young children and of interest to boys and girls alike. They range from basic to more complex, with the selection depending on the teacher's understanding of the interests, needs, and developmental levels of the children.

In all of the themes, establish a literacy-enriched environment by including materials such as related picture books, children's magazines to read, a phone book, and small pads, paper, index cards, pencils, alphabet stamps, and envelopes to write lists, receipts, labels, notes, letters, and stories. Paper clips, a paper punch, tape, and rulers are also useful and children can be taught how to manage a stapler safely. Post identifying signs (Open, Closed, Entrance, Exit, Post Office) and supply washable magic markers and various sizes of paper so children can make their own signs or a "taking turns" chart. Morrow (1990) found that providing literacy materials in dramatic play areas increases such preschool behaviors as paper handling, reading, and writing. Later research by Morrow and Schickedanz (2006, p.275) "demonstrated that adult support for literacy-enriched dramatic play, *provided outside of the play itself*, can have beneficial effects on children's literacy-related play behaviors."

Other initial basic props need not be extensive because new items can be introduced from time to time to maintain interest. For example, add some food coupons and newspaper advertisements to the grocery theme or a new section for frozen foods. Consider also the special needs and concerns in the group. Would a brace, arm sling, walking cane, or a sound amplifier worn around the neck represent the diversity of the classroom? Dramatic play room materials also need to reflect the students' cultures and experiences.

House theme

- table, chairs, and refrigerator can be made from cardboard boxes with painted details

- dishes, utensils, plastic food

- doll bed, large baby dolls of different ethnicities, and size 12-months infant clothing donated by parents

- easy-to-put-on dress-ups such as jackets, hats, and purses, briefcase, toolbox, and lunchbox

- small suitcase.

Grocery theme

- empty food boxes stuffed with crumpled newspaper and taped shut, empty cans with masking tape around opened edges

- plastic fruit and vegetables

- table for checkout

- calculator and/or cash register made from boxes with painted details, play money, price labels

- picture/word signs showing cost of items, paper and pencils

- store baskets and cloth bags for carry-out.

Restaurant theme

- table, chairs, placemats, dishes, napkins, plastic utensils

- large pictures of healthy foods

- picture/word menu listing items which the children have selected and discussed

- play food or pretend food drawn on white paper plates

- pad and pencils for orders and guest checks, play money, calculator or adding machine, play credit card and a credit card machine made from a cardboard box with painted details.

Figure 3.1: McDonald's Restaurant

Different versions of the restaurant might include a fast-food restaurant, an ice cream shop, or a pizza parlor. These restaurants can offer cardboard hamburgers or ice cream cones made from yarn pompom balls in foam cups. Pizzas and trimmings can be made from circles of cardboard cut into serving sections. One-half sections and one-fourth sections are more understandable when you see and separate a whole pizza into parts.

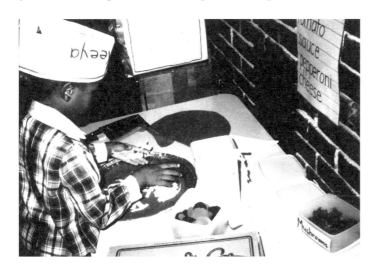

Figure 3.2: The Pizza Parlor

Fire station theme

- plastic fire hats, small plastic ponchos, boots
- telephone, bell
- large box for the fire truck with painted details and a steering wheel, or use several rows of chairs
- four-foot (120 cm) length of garden hose, flashlights
- crumpled red cellophane paper for the fire
- dolls to be saved from the fire.

Post office theme

- table, paper and pencils, stamps and ink pad, envelopes, paste, stamps to sell. Parents can donate advertising stamps received in the mail or stamps cut from mailings
- class name list with photos
- picture/word cost signs, "Open" and "Closed" signs

- boxes to mail that are taped shut, address labels

- adding machine, play money

- homemade mail box, mail carrier hat and bag

- labeled shoe box or folder for each child to receive mail.

Bakery theme

FRONT STORE FOR SALES

- cookies, small cakes, and pies, made in the rear bakery

- cash register, paper and pencils, play money, paper bags

- picture/word cost signs.

REAR AREA FOR BAKING

- Children make bakery items using: homemade play dough (see Figure 3.3)

- aprons, paper chef hats

- pretend bakery items made from homemade dough and other materials such as circles cut from light cardboard for cookies, and larger circles and rectangles cut from thin Styrofoam® for cakes and pies

- oven made from a cardboard box with painted details, cookie cutters, spatula, oven mitts, baking trays

- crayons, magic markers, poster paint, brushes for decorating items.

Figure 3.3: The Bakery, front and rear

> ## Homemade play dough recipe
>
> 1 cup of flour
>
> ½ cup of salt
>
> ⅓ to ½ cup of water or enough to form the dough
>
> Optional: food coloring
>
> Mix together.
>
> Homemade dough will keep for several days in a plastic bag in a refrigerator. One tablespoon of powdered alum (available at drug stores) can be added as a preservative.

Doctor's office theme

WAITING AREA

- desk and chair for receptionist, phone, sign-in sheet, paper and pencils, play money, magazines, appointment calendar.

EXAMINING AREA

- stethoscope, white shirts with sleeves cut for examining coats, rubber gloves, penlight, pad for prescriptions

- bathroom scale, height chart, arm sling, band aids, strips of cloth used for bandages, tape, paper masks, old x-ray pictures

- large baby doll patients

- examining table

- small pads for prescriptions and billing.

This theme can easily be changed to a dentist's office by removing unnecessary items (e.g. stethoscope, scale and bandages) and adding others, such as a sturdy chair for examinations, individual straws for viewing inside the mouth, a small hand mirror, and perhaps simple drawings of proper brushing created by an artistic parent.

Veterinarian's office theme

- variety of small and medium toy animals

- pet collars, name tags, and leashes

- open cardboard boxes to house animals who need to stay

- reception desk, phone, examining table

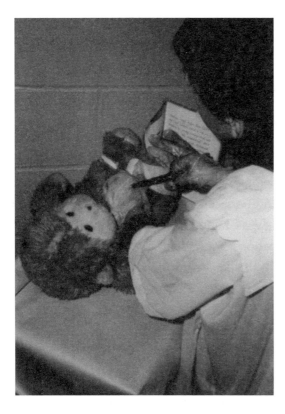

Figure 3.4: The Veterinarian's Office

- paper masks, old white shirts with sleeves cut for examining coats

- plastic pet dishes

- cotton balls, bandages and tape, Q-tips, pretend thermometer, magnifying glass, plastic eye dropper

- pet combs and brushes

- play money, clipboard, paper and pencils.

Repair shop theme

- variety of small appliances with electrical cords removed

- work table, tool box with small hammer, regular and Phillips screwdriver, pliers, bendable wire, tape, nuts and bolts, penlight

- apron, safety glasses, measuring tape, folding rule

- telephone, pad and pencils, adding machine, cash register, play money.

Figure 3.5: The Repair Shop

Numerous other dramatic play settings can be developed and integrated with the children's study of the wider community. Some examples are:

- the drug or book store
- flower shop
- library
- unisex hair salon
- gas station
- bank
- hospital
- airport
- newspaper office
- space program.

Another approach could be to establish a dramatic play area to adapt a familiar story such as *The City Mouse and the Country Mouse*. A few related props can be placed in the dramatic play area with the announcement, "Now, let's see what else could happen in the story," sharing the new storyline with the class. Novel dramatic play themes enable young children to practice skills in an appealing way that invites innovation.

Figure 3.6: The Laundromat

Figure 3.7: Depositing money at the bank

Figure 3.8: The Airport

Figure 3.9: The Airport ticket counter

OBSERVING DRAMATIC PLAY SKILLS

In general, as children become more experienced in managing dramatic play, the teacher becomes less involved in guiding it. This provides time for more continuous observing which can help identify each child's current strengths and needs. The goal of observing, however, is actually to *use* this insight in planning teaching strategies that enhance the children's development. Using planning as the basis for observing ensures that information is not just randomly collected, filed, and forgotten. It is applied and can help young children adapt to new experiences.

There are a variety of ways of observing overall behavior, but simplicity tends to ensure that observing and recording will be done on a consistent basis. Teachers usually begin to gather general or "anecdotal information" early in the year to build a working understanding of each child. Keeping track of observations in a busy classroom, however, can be challenging. A helpful way to start is to use a small notebook with a pencil attached and during the day note "significant happenings" or incidents that for some reason attract your curiosity and attention. Often while observing dramatic play, you will find yourself reasoning "I need to remember this." Jot down the child's name and a few words to help recall the incident. These notes and your reflections can then be transferred to individual name cards which are regularly reviewed and used in planning. Does the child need a friend, an assigned task to talk about, or more recognition of her/his ideas? Dramatic play observations are especially useful to the teacher in planning for individual needs. This type of anecdotal observing is also manageable because it need not be done daily for each child but rather for notable items. Be alert to children with repeated behavior patterns that may indicate an interest, ability, or concern, as well as children who have few or no recorded observations. These quiet ones can be easily overlooked but may need supportive intervention. Also include positive comments about things that are going well. This enables you to comment about the incident either privately, to the group, or to parents, capitalizing on the positive recognition and encouragement.

To supplement this, teachers can also adapt the following questions to design their own checklist for on-the-spot assessment of individual dramatic play skills. A selected range, such as Frequently/Occasionally/Not Yet; or 1 (lowest) to 5 (highest), can be used to record the performance level. Sometimes a Yes/No response is sufficient, but for other items, thoughts for future planning can be added.

DRAMATIC PLAY SKILLS

- Does she initiate the play?

- Does he always play with the same children?

- Can she make-believe with objects?

- Can he improvise if an object is not available?

- How often does she verbalize?

- Is his vocabulary limited or varied?

- What level of vocabulary does she use?

- Does he encourage others to join the play?

- Does she contribute ideas to the play?

- Does he perform the actions and activities of the assumed role?

- Does she introduce events or ideas that flow in a meaningful manner or tend to wander about?

- Does he seek adult intervention often?

- How does she respond to suggestions?

- How long does he stay in a role?

Of course, these are only suggestions. The teacher needs to be the designer as each child is different, each class is different, and each grade level is different. Still, the basic question for the teacher remains the same: What does the teacher need to know to plan strategies to advance learning? The beauty of a checklist is that it can be designed to spotlight what *you* want to observe.

Now, with dramatic play underway and thriving, what other everyday drama activities can be used to involve children in pretending and prepare them for story dramatizations?

Chapter 4

CAMERA: ADDING STORY PRETENDING AND DRAMA TO EVERYDAY ACTIVITIES

DRAMA AND STORIES

Everyday classroom activities can often be adapted to include story pretending and drama, but too frequently these opportunities are overlooked or unrecognized. This section is designed to help teachers introduce and extend drama by using stories in mimes, finger plays, nursery rhymes, poems, and picture books, and suggests related resource books to adapt and expand these ideas.

In planning a story pretending activity, consider certain questions: Does the story involved lend itself to dramatization? Does it have action, dramatic effect, and appeal? These are basic necessities for young children with a special emphasis on action. Begin with whole-group involvement as it is often easier to pretend when others are pretending with you. Most story forms can be first read engagingly by the teacher and then reread with volunteers speaking some dialogue. Next, you might suggest, "Let's pretend this nursery rhyme is really happening. You can act it out and I'll read the story." Then ask the children for *their* ideas: "How could you pretend to be a clock? How would you pretend to climb a clock? What kind of noise could a clock make when it strikes? How can we make a noise like that?" New vocabulary will need to be defined *with* the children, used in conjunction with more familiar words, and linked to their own experiences. Using new words frequently is another major aspect of vocabulary building. Acting out new words is also important as it provides children with concrete examples to extend their understanding of the words. Vocabulary words can also be written on index cards (preceded when appropriate by a picture) for use as a reference when writing.

Story pretending need not be elaborate and should be simple and brief, especially when beginning. A touch of drama can even be slipped into classroom work at random times for relaxation. Pretending time can be planned to involve the whole group, individuals, pairs, or small and medium-sized groups. Often only a favorite section of a story will be dramatized, although older children sometimes like to be involved in the whole story during a rereading. At this point, they are really approaching "doing" an actual story dramatization but without the staging, props, and costumes. Including drama in everyday activities can certainly give young children an expanded view of what telling a story is all about.

Mime

Mime is a delightful way to introduce young children to using actions to express their ideas. By focusing on body movements and facial gestures rather than words, they have an opportunity to expand and polish their pretending skills. In addition, creative thinking is emphasized and mime appeals to nearly everyone, including English language learners, children from diverse cultural backgrounds, and children with special needs. Non-verbal, language-delayed, and children with other communication concerns welcome mime as a means of participating physically and sharing their ideas. By watching others use mime, children can observe different ways of presenting ideas and learn to accept and respect individuality in interpretations and others. By interacting with knowledgeable others, children explore more complex ideas and how to portray them. The timing of mime is also adjustable so it can be slipped into transition gaps such as waiting for the bus or lunch to arrive.

Younger children initially benefit from discussing and modeling to help them visualize the movements involved. *Their* movements, however, should reflect *their* thinking, and individual interpretations need to be noticed and valued. As they feel more skillful, ask them to suggest new ideas they would like to act out. For beginning mime, some of the following might be used:

- drinking a glass of milk
- eating an ice cream cone
- washing your hands
- combing your hair
- opening an umbrella
- walking in a puddle
- pushing a wagon
- sweeping with a broom
- shoveling snow
- digging a hole
- putting on a snow jacket
- putting on snow pants
- pulling a sled.

The ability to mime grows as children gain experience in investigating different ways of representing familiar ideas. More experienced children find the following mimes challenging:

- painting a wall
- hammering a nail
- sawing a piece of wood
- shooting a basket ball
- dribbling a basket ball
- playing hockey
- rowing a boat
- flying a kite
- three children jumping rope
- swimming across a pool
- figure ice skating
- riding a merry-go-round.

After mastering a basic mime, the children can add other related actions such as climbing on the merry-go-round horse or waving to a friend as they ride. You might ask, "How do you move to climb on the horse? What could you do while you are riding?" A phrase can also be suggested for the children to act out such as, "I'm really happy (*smile and hug yourself*)," "That's awful (*make a face and cringe*)," or "I'm going to hide (*crouch down and cover you head with your arms*)." Older children often enjoy a little complexity by breaking a basic mime into a number of smaller parts. First, you turn on the water, rub your hands on the soap, rub your hands together, rinse off the water, turn off the faucet, and dry your hands. Each mime can be quite unique.

Children can use mime to pretend being a favorite animal such as a trotting horse, an upright and growling bear, a bird bringing food to a nest, or a curled-up, sleepy kitten. They will also enjoy playing *Show and Guess* in which a child mimes an idea and the others try to guess the action. If there are problems guessing, more hints can be provided.

Finger plays

Another way to practice pretending is through finger plays. These focus mainly on hand and finger movements and have a brief, catchy verse to recite that accompanies the action. As they appeal to groups, teachers have long used them to gather children together, gain and direct their attention, and ease waiting periods. As some verses include counting, they can also be used to reinforce math concepts. Many finger plays, however, have clever storylines and are adaptable to dramatization.

Usually, the teacher models the verse and actions and then the group joins the activity each in their own way. The topic and vocabulary should be familiar so the children can follow the storyline, and the wording is initially slower paced to allow time to coordinate the words and actions. Even the youngest enjoy pretending to be a train, and talking about the centerfold illustration in Donald Crews' book *Freight Train* (1998) can be an interesting follow-up activity.

The Train (Author unknown)

The choo choo train goes up the track.
(run fingers up extended arm)
It says, WOOO, WOOO,
and it comes right back.
(run fingers down the extended arm)

Simple finger plays about animal antics are often amusing and especially when the children know about the animal's habits. For the following, a pet turtle might pay an extended visit to the class and stimulate scientific investigation.

 My turtle (Author unknown)

Here is my pet turtle.
(make a fist; extend thumb)
He lives in a shell,
(hide thumb in fist)
And he likes this house very, very well.
He pokes his head out when he want to eat,
(extend thumb and wiggle)
And pulls it back in when he wants to sleep.
(hide thumb in fist)

The following finger play is a long time winner.

 The Rabbit (Author unknown)

Here is the bunny with ears so funny,
(hold up two fingers to make a "V")
And here is his home in the ground,
(touch index and thumb fingers of other hand to make an "O" for the home)
When a noise he hears, he wiggles his ears,
(wiggle "V" fingers)
and he jumps into the ground.

After performing the finger play, children can enjoy acting it out. Several volunteers can pretend to be bunnies and improvise the action with their bodies while the other children recite the verse. Sound effects can be added by asking, "What kind of sound can we make when the rabbit hears a noise?" A chalk dot on the floor or non-sliding carpet squares can indicate rabbit holes.

Add variety by including some seasonal finger plays.

 Autumn leaves (Author unknown)

Autumn leaves are falling down,
(wiggle fingers from above head to floor)
All brown and yellow, green and red.
They fall softly like the rain,
(tap fingers on the floor)

WOOOOPS!
 (clap)
One landed on my head!
 (tap fingers on head)

Optional lines:
Let's rake them in a pile so high
 (spread fingers and pretend to rake leaves)
Look up! They nearly touch the sky!
 (look up and reach both arms up high)

After learning the finger play, children can examine and talk about different kinds of common leaves (more science) and make their own pretend paper leaves for a prop box. The teacher can recite the verse as a child, perhaps in a wheelchair, scatters the leaves in the air as the others move in their own way to dramatize the verse. "What happens when a wind blows through?" Appropriate music such as track 10 (Deux Arabesques 1) from the disc *Debussy for Daydreaming* (1995) adds a pleasant background for pretending, and the children can use their whole body to represent leaves floating in the air. When the music stops, they flutter to the ground. Try other variations such as sitting on the floor and the children lifting their arms up as high as they can stretch and slowly lowering their bodies like falling leaves.

Physically challenged children can lower their hands, their head, or upper body. Of course, when all the leaves have been raked into one pile, the children will probably need to jump into it. This type of active dramatization requires an open space in the room or perhaps in the gym or outdoors, and a few safety considerations.

Finger plays can also introduce and dramatize a theme the class is studying, such as learning about growing plants. Of course, the next step is to plant some flowers such as marigolds which are extremely sturdy and forgiving.

 ## My Garden (Author unknown)

Here is my garden.
 (hold out one hand, palm up)
I'll rake it with care.
 (rake palm with fingers of other hand)
And then I'll plant my flower seeds in there.
 (pretend to sprinkle flower seeds on palm)
And the sun will shine,
 (make a circle with arms)
and the rain will fall,
 (flutter fingers down)
and my flowers will grow, straight and tall.
 (flutter finger up)

Finger plays can also include pretending holiday observations. Who could resist this Halloween action?

 Surprise! (Author unknown)

> See my big and scary eyes.
>> *(make circles with thumb and index fingers around both eyes)*
> Be ready now for a big surprise
>> *(cover face with both hands, then quickly remove them)*
> BOO!

"Now, who knows another way to pretend to be scary?"

FAVORITE BOOKS OF FINGER PLAYS (AND RECORDINGS) FOR PRETENDING

Grayson, M. (1988) *Let's Do Fingerplays*. Pittsburgh, PA: Dorrance Publishing Co.

Mohrma, G. and the Totline Staff (2001) *1001 Rhymes and Fingerplays*. Waldoboro, ME. Totline Publications.

Silberg, J. and Schiller, P. (2002) *The Complete Book of Rhymes, Songs, Poems, Finger Plays and Chants*. Betsville, MD: Gryphon House.

RELATED REFERENCES

Crews, D. (1998) *Freight Train*. New York, NY: HarperCollins.

Debussy for Daydreaming, Track 10 (Deux Arabesque 1) (1995) New York, NY: Philips Classics.

Nursery rhymes and poems

With a little imagination and innovation, nursery rhymes and poems can provide different opportunities to explore pretending. After reading them, the teacher might suggest simple word changes that can be dramatized, and soon the children will be offering ideas of their own.

A familiar nursery rhyme such as "Little Miss Muffet" (Scarry 1999) can provide a good beginning. It has rhyme, rhythm, and action and clearly illustrates that a storyline has a beginning, middle, and end. The quaint vocabulary will need to be explained and basic props can be added. "What could we use for a tuffet?" If a small stool is not available, use a sturdy cardboard box and pretend it's a tuffet. "What do you think curds and whey taste like?" (They are similar to cottage cheese.) "What might Miss Muffet wear? How would the spider crawl to frighten her?" By acting out the rhyme and adding some visual details, the story comes alive and the children *experience* drama. To extend the pretending, a temporary Miss Muffet dramatic play spot with a few props could be established. Of course, the children would negotiate and adapt the story on their own. They might decide to have several spiders moving about, or maybe a grizzly bear and her cubs would saunter in and frighten the lady. This type of creative innovation can also be shared with the class.

Another nursery rhyme available for later adaptation and dramatization is "Hickory, dickory dock" (traditional) which contains repetition, play on words, and lots of nonsense together with the storyline. When the children know the rhyme, add a touch of drama.

 ## Hickory, dickory dock (traditional)

Hickory, dickory dock.
The mouse ran up the clock.
   *(one child is the clock and another flutters fingers from
   the bottom to the top of the clock child)*
The clock struck one,
   (clap hands, or strike triangle once)
The mouse ran down.
   *(the mouse child flutters fingers from the top to the
   bottom of the clock child)*
Hickory, dickory dock.

The players can be changed to involve more children and basic props such as a paper clock face with moveable hands (adding some math), and a clothesline

mouse tail might be added. For additional pretending, recite and dramatize some new lines. Talk about how words can sound the same and that if we listen carefully, we can begin to hear words that sound the same. The teacher might offer some examples but as the children really begin to listen and hear the sounds of the words involved, they will enjoy creating and dramatizing their own endings for this rhyme. Some suggestions might include:

The clock struck one.
Out came the sun.
   (child forms large circle with arms above head)
or
The clock struck two.
The mouse dropped a shoe.
   (mouse child drops one shoe)
or
The clock struck three.
The mouse rubbed his knee.
   (mouse child rubs knee)

Still another nursery rhyme that is quite open to dramatization and alterations is "Hey, diddle diddle" (Scarry 1999). A cat can pretend to play the violin, a cow can jump over a medium-sized ball representing the moon, a dog can laugh and jump up and down, and a dish can sing a tune to a spoon. The chorus, in turn, simply adjusts the lines accordingly. All it takes to dramatize action nursery rhymes is imagination and a sense of humor, and young children certainly have both.

Other nursery rhymes children enjoy dramatizing (and adapting) as a group include:

- Humpty Dumpty
- Jack, Be Nimble
- Little Boy Blue
- Little Jack Horner
- Sing a Song of Sixpence
- Three Little Kittens.

FAVORITE BOOKS OF NURSERY RHYMES FOR PRETENDING

Hague, M. (1984) *Mother Goose: A Collection of Classic Nursery Rhymes.* New York, NY: Henry Holt and Co.

Scarry, R. (1999) *Best Mother Goose Ever.* New York, NY: Golden Books Publishing Company.

Wright, B.F. (1994) *The Real Mother Goose.* New York, NY: Scholastic.

Poetry

Poetry is usually viewed as a relaxing reading and listening endeavor but when linked with drama, its potential benefits are noteworthy. Poetry, like mime, rhymes, and stories, can help clarify story content and meaning and introduce unfamiliar vocabulary. Dramatizing poetry enables children to further explore sounds, rhyme, rhythm, and humor, and to internalize language by pretending to be in situations that seem realistic. Basic emotional ideas, opinions, and attitudes can be explored and communication sharpened by facial gestures and body movements. Poetry comes alive when children listen and visualize the words, discuss and understand their meaning, and then use actions to portray them. Shel Silverstein's poem *Safe* (1996) combines a good beginning poem with a safety lesson. After reading the poem, talk about the importance of crossing a street safely by looking left and right for cars. Then place two strips of colored tape parallel to each other on the floor to indicate a street and the class can enjoy pretending the poem as you reread it. The children can stand along one side of the street and perhaps shuffle their feet as they look left and right to check traffic. When everyone agrees it is safe to cross, off they march to the other side.

Now, add some other ideas. When you look left, point your foot left too, and do the same when you look right. How about also pointing your arm? Several children could pretend to drive cars (moving hands on the steering wheel) down the street with the walkers responding correctly. A horn beep might be added. Ask the children for other ideas such as holding hands as they walk across. Older children might like the challenge of dividing into two groups and crossing from opposite sides. Facing left and right can then become a challenge.

The following poem by Kathleen Fraser (Fraser 1968; Prelutsky 1983) offers still more pretending and challenges.

Broom Balancing

Millicent can play the flute
And Francine can dance a jig,
But I can balance a broom.
Susanna knows how to make cookies
And Harold can stand on one foot.
But I can balance a broom.

Jeffry can climb a ladder backwards
And Andrew can count to five thousand two,
But I can balance a broom.
Do you think a circus might discover me?

First, introduce the poem by providing background knowledge about any unfamiliar words like "flute" or "jig." Then read the poem aloud and enjoy its rhythm and gentle humor. Talk about the poem and the different interesting accomplishments. Which action do you like best? How could you pretend you're baking cookies? Now it's time for some activity! Provide a child-size broom or a short fireplace broom with a sturdy handle and invite volunteers to try broom balancing. After practicing read the poem again, pausing to encourage volunteers to dramatize some of the accomplishments, each in their own individual way. While young children are generally great at hopping about and dancing a jig, pretending to climb a ladder backwards could be difficult. In this case simply adapt the poem by changing the words and actions. For example, walking backwards could be quite manageable and children can always select a number to count rather than contemplating five thousand and two.

At another time children might enjoy reworking the poem by substituting their own names and talents for the original ones. A volunteer could narrate while others dramatize this new version–the activity might even extend to creating a class book complete with illustrations. In a related activity children can think of additional unbreakable objects to balance, such as a plastic soda bottle. Compare balancing an empty bottle with one half-full of water and science is involved. A parent might also take photographs of the children pretending an action so that each can talk, draw, dictate or write about their photograph and share their accomplishments with friends and family.

FAVORITE BOOKS OF POEMS FOR PRETENDING

De Regniers, B. (1989) *Sing a Song of Popcorn: Every Child's Book of Poems.* New York, NY: Scholastic.

dePaola, T. (1988) *Tomie dePaola's Book of Poems.* New York, NY: G.P. Putman's Sons.

Prelutsky, J. (1983) *The Random House Book of Poetry for Children.* New York, NY: Random House.

Silverstein, S. (1996) *Falling Up.* New York, NY: HarperCollins.

Picture storybooks

Certain picture storybooks become class favorites and are requested to be read again and again. Among these, folk tales are often perfect for pretending as they are familiar and offer considerable action, suspense, and appeal. While hearing one retold, children can join the fun and portray parts of the action as the teacher narrates. One can easily slip into the role of the Gingerbread Man and experience the excitement of being chased and calling out those famous lines: "Run, run, as fast as you can. You *can't* catch me. I'm the Gingerbread Man!" (Schmidt 1985). Several children can be involved as there are a number of animal characters, and a chorus can join in the repetitive phrases. After dramatizing the original version, older children might plan to change the story to a novel setting, perhaps at the zoo. This challenge can stimulate some highly original and sometimes humorous ideas. The Gingerbread Man might hop out of the zookeeper's lunchbox, be chased by a number of interesting animals, such as a lion, a gorilla, or a spider, before meeting an obliging alligator who offers to take him across a pond. "What other animals might chase him? How can we change how the story ends?" Then act out parts of the new version. To further extend the pretending, compare several versions of *The Gingerbread Man*, and talk about similarities and differences both in the text and illustrations. This could help children visualize different possibilities in settings, characters, dialogue, and events and extend their comprehension. Try pretending sections of a more unique version. The following variations would be interesting to explore:

Schmidt, K. (1985) *The Gingerbread Man*. New York, NY: Scholastic.
Galdone, P. (1975) *The Gingerbread Boy*. New York, NY: Houghton Mifflin Company.
Amoss, B. (1994) *The Cajun Gingerbread Boy*. New Orleans, LA: MTC Press.
Kimmel, E. (1993) *The Gingerbread Man*. New York, NY: Holiday House.

Certain folk or nursery tales have delighted generations of children because they are fine stories that convey valuable lessons to think about. You can always adapt a version you feel might be upsetting—for example, in *Red Riding Hood* have Grandmother hide in a closet and *not* be eaten by the wolf. All-time favorite folk tales include:

- *Red Riding Hood*
- *The Little Red Hen*
- *The Three Bears*
- *The Lion and the Mouse*
- *The Three Little Pigs*
- *The Gingerbread Man*.

After reading these classics experiment with different pretending activities. *Red Riding Hood* might become a temporary dramatic play area with the addition of a few simple props. Several children could decide how to change a favorite story, act it out, and then share their new version with the group. For example, after reading *The Lion and the Mouse*, they might have Mickey Mouse fall into a trap and then solve how brave Minnie Mouse or Pluto could rescue him. The teacher's comments and questions can help to stimulate thinking: "What's a 'trap'? What would Mickey say when he found he was in a trap? How do you think his voice would sound? What could Minnie do to help him get out?"

Stories other than folk tales provide many opportunities to practice pretending and later dramatize. *Caps for Sale* (Slobodkina 1940) is a wonderful picture book which always charms a group of children. It offers action and subtle humor, and everybody can be involved as the teacher reads to the group. Each can pretend to be a member of the humorous monkey band, sitting in a pretend tree and wearing the pretend caps the peddler needs to sell to his customers. Angrily, a volunteer playing the peddler shakes his finger and exclaims, "You monkeys you, you give me back my caps," but the monkeys only shake their fingers back at him, responding, "Tsz, tsz, tsz." Then the action escalates as the peddler shakes both hands and stamps both feet, repeating his demand. Each time the children can respond by doing the same action back to him, and calling, "Tsz, tsz, tsz." Only when the peddler throws his cap on the ground do the monkeys throw their pretend caps on the ground. Then the peddler collects his caps, places them on his head, and goes on his way, looking for people to buy them. What a fun opportunity to practice pretending! Consider also the vocabulary possibilities: peddler, wares, checkered cap, customers, bunch, tree trunk, fifty cents, refreshed, left, right, in back, behind. Initially, it also helps comprehension to explain that monkeys like to do the same things they see others do and introduce the word "imitate."

The class can also go outside to pretend. After having an opportune snowfall, read Keats's *The Snowy Day* (1976) and pretend some of Peter's adventures. The children can pretend to be Peter and walk with their feet pointing out and pointing in or build a snowman or make angels in the snow. If you don't have snow in your area, pretend walking in snow inside. "How could Peter make different tracks in the snow with his feet?" The children might try walking on their tiptoes, on their heels, backwards, or with one foot right in front of the other. How about hopping tracks? "How could you tell by the track in the snow that Peter was hopping?" An agile visiting parent might even outline examples of the footprints on paper using a magic marker. What an opportune time to talk about how Native Americans use tracks to learn things. "What could you learn from looking at a footprint?"

A number of picture books can add a multicultural flavor to pretending. Ichikawa's endearing story *The*

First Bear in Africa (2001) relates how a little girl visitor from far away loses her teddy bear in Africa and how a local boy named Metro and his animal friends race through the savannah to return it to her. The story offers opportunities for integrated learning, whether acting out sections and rotating roles or dramatizing the entire story. After reading and discussing the story, older children can compile a chart list of characters using the Swahili names of the animals provided in the rear of the book. Imagine the fun of knowing that *twiga* means a giraffe in Swahili and *simba* means a lion. The children can even learn to say goodbye, *kwaheri*. Make copies and label pictures of the main animals in the book (hippopotamus, lion, elephant, and giraffe) to help in sequencing the story. These pictures can be displayed in their order of appearance during the retelling. Several props can be used, such as a teddy bear with a red bow or a colorful scarf for Metro to tie over his shoulder. Paper-plate masks which are held (p.134) can be created to represent the animals and add a touch of realism.

Segments of wordless picture books such as *Pancakes for Breakfast* (dePaola 1978) can also be mimed by one child while another picture-reads the illustrations. Then as pages are turned, a different mimer and picture reader can swing into action.

FAVORITE PICTURE BOOKS FOR PRETENDING

Bret, J. (1989) *The Mitten: A Ukrainian Folklore*. New York, NY: Scholastic.

Brown, M.W. (1974) *Good Night Moon*. New York, NY: Harper and Row.

Brown, M.W. (1956) *The Runaway Bunny*. New York, NY: Harper and Row.

Brown, M.W. (1989) *Home for a Bunny*. New York, NY: Random House.

Christelow, E. (1989) *Five Little Monkeys Jumping on the Bed*. New York, NY: Clarion Books.

Cowley, J. (1980) *Mrs. Wishy Washy*. Bothwell, WA: The Wright Group.

dePaola, T. (1978) *Pancakes for Breakfast*. New York, NY: Scholastic.

Scarry, R. (1999) *Best Mother Goose Ever*. New York, NY: Golden Books Publishing Company.

Eastman, P. (1960) *Are You My Mother?* Cleveland, OH: William Collins and Sons.

Engelbreit, M. (2008) *Mary Engelbreit's Nursery Tales: A Treasury of Children's Classics*. New York, NY: HarperCollins.

Galdone, P. (1984) *The Elves and the Shoemaker*. New York, NY: Carion Books.

Galdone, P. (2011) *The Little Red Hen*. Boston, MA: Houghton Mifflin Harcourt.

Galdone, P. (2011) *The Three Bears*. Boston, MA: Houghton Mifflin Harcourt.

Galdone, P. (2011) *The Three Little Pigs*. Boston, MA: Houghton Mifflin Harcourt.

Hutchins, P. (1989) *The Doorbell Rang*. New York, NY: Greenwillow Books.

Ichikawa, S. (2001) *The First Bear in Africa*. New York, NY: Philomel Books.

Keats, E.J. (1976) *The Snowy Day*. New York, NY: Puffin Books.

Kimmel, E. (1988) *Anansi and the Moss-Covered Rock*. New York, NY: Scholastic.

Kimmel, E. (1993) *The Gingerbread Man*. New York, NY: Holiday House.

McGovern, A. (1986) *Stone Soup*. New York, NY: Scholastic.

McGovern, A. (1967) *Too Much Noise*. Boston, MA: Houghton Mifflin.

Morgan, P. (1990) *The Turnip: An Old Russian Folktale*. New York, NY: Scholastic.

Pickney, J. (2009) *The Lion and the Mouse*. New York, NY: Little, Brown.

Ransom, C. (2002) *Little Red Riding Hood*. Columbus, OH: School Specialty Publishing.

Sendak, M. (1962) *Chicken Soup with Rice*. New York, NY: Scholastic.

Sendak, M. (1963) *Where the Wild Things Are*. New York, NY: Harper and Row.

Slobodkina, E. (1940) *Caps for Sale*. New York, NY: W.R. Scott.

DRAMA AND ART

Drama and art can be natural partners in a number of everyday classroom activities that enable young children to represent their thoughts, emotions, and knowledge. By experimenting with various possibilities, a number of imaginative ways can be uncovered to combine story pretending and drama with representational art forms in a meaningful way for children.

To practice pretending, you might begin with some colorful, eye-catching magazine advertisements. Save large pictures that illustrate various emotions—for example, happy, sad, angry, surprised, frightened. Share them with the children and together *read* the facial expressions: "How do you think this person feels? What makes this face look happy? Can you pretend to make your face look happy, sad or tired? Could you paint a picture of your face when it looks happy?" A hand-held mirror can provide a helpful reference.

As children become involved in pretending nursery rhymes, poems, and picture storybooks, they are often motivated to draw or paint a favorite story event or portray a character in clay or with a handmade puppet. Children can use their imagination to create simple accessories to dramatize parts of a retold story. For example, in Slobodkina's tale *Caps for Sale* (1940), children pretending to be monkeys can design sturdy paper plates to represent caps which are worn and thrown to the ground during the retelling. After listening to Margaret Wise Brown's charming story *Goodnight Moon*

(1974), younger children might draw or paint their favorite toy to hug and tell good night, and perhaps volunteer to act out the scene.

Later, when preparing to dramatize a story, even more art opportunities become available. Small groups of children might draw different story sections on large sheets of paper which are then assembled to make a mural of the story. They may need a little guidance in deciding the contents of each section, but the drawings should contain their own imaginative ideas. In the nursery tale *The Three Bears* (2011), the groups might use magic markers to illustrate three sections, such as the bears leaving the house in the woods, the bears finding the empty bowls and broken chairs, and Goldilocks sound asleep in Baby Bear's bed. Volunteers might then casually act out the event in each section of the mural. The composite work could then be hung in the hallway outside the room to be admired by those passing by. Older children might prefer to paint their own individual scene from the story and dictate or write an accompanying text to portray with friends to the class. Others could contribute a few homemade props or draw simple costumes for the characters and also

share their ideas. Not only is teamwork and decision making involved, but the children also gain experience in planning characters, objects, and events of the story.

Pictures and artists

Certain art works are especially appealing to children, and looking and talking about them provides a natural way to imagine the possible stories involved. Art and drama can be combined both in focused group activities or during brief time intervals such as before lunch or during a transition. In the process, children benefit by becoming aware of the beauty around them and learning to think about it, enjoy it and take happiness from it.

Gradually throughout the year, introduce some beautiful and interesting paintings by using the large-size reproductions in the books listed on p.83. These books are usually available at most local libraries or can be easily obtained through inter-library loan. Books of favorite reproductions might be included in room supply orders or perhaps requested as a donation from the school PTA. Often museums sell poster reproductions fairly inexpensively which can be put on the classroom walls at the children's eye level. For easy reference, when an art work is referred to in this section, the name of the author or book title and page number of the reproduction is given. The series of books on individual artists *Getting to Know the World's Great Artists* by Mike Venezia contains pictures of a variety of well-known reproductions along with information about the artists which children find appealing.

By viewing and discussing a piece of art, children begin to think about the story it can convey and how artists use different methods to tell stories. Artists can draw, use paint, colored paper, wood, clay, and a variety of other materials to represent their ideas. Becoming familiar with an artist's style helps children realize that what the artist *saw* and *how* the completed work looked can be very different. Knowing that ideas can be expressed in different ways tends to assure children that it's OK to paint things their own way.

Look and talk about the setting, people, clothing, and other details of a painting of interest to children. Discuss how artists had to really think about *what* and *how* they wanted to paint the picture. Consider Monet's lovely work *Waterlily Pond* (*The Art Book for Children,*

Book One, p.69), with its Japanese-style bridge and lily pond which convey the peacefulness of a bright summer day and suggests the staging for a story. "Who do you think could walk over this bridge? What animals might be in the water? What might happen next?" The imagined story might be basic and brief but it can also be acted out. Older children might paint *their* story about the bridge or pretend they are Monet repainting this masterpiece *but in their very own individual way*. Some might like to imitate Monet, using little dabs of paint and blending soft colors together. Others, after viewing van Gogh's, *Sunflowers*, (Venezia 1988, van Gogh, p.26), might prefer to use thick paints and bright colors.

Andy Warhol's painting *Big Campbell's Soup Can* (Sayre 2004, p.87) is very different because it is of a common, everyday object that children will easily recognize. The children can enjoy comparing how the painting differs from a real can of Campbell's beef noodle soup, and realize that common items can suggest a good story to pretend. "Think of something in your room at home that you would like to paint? Your new shoes? What could you pretend happens to those shoes?"

The bold colors, shapes and forms used by Henry Matisse in his work *The Snail* (Welton 2002, p.39) often intrigues children. Matisse studied a real snail in his hand and then created the picture with paper cut-outs, using bright colors. If possible, examine a live snail or an informative picture of one. Then examine the painting: "Can you find a snail in the picture? What do you think the snail could be doing? You could pretend to be Matisse and make your own picture of a snail."

The story in Jacob Lawrence's painting *The Migration of the Negro No. 32* (Sayre 2004, p.81) presents its own tale to share with the children. Years ago (World War II), African American people had to wait a long time for trains to take them places where the family could find good jobs. "How do you think the boy on the suitcase feels waiting so long for his train? What might he be thinking? What could he and the others do while waiting?" How about singing a song? You might change the lyrics of an old favorite "If you're happy and you know it" by singing, "If you're very tired of waiting, clap your hands/slap your knees/jump up and down." It may initially take a little prompting, but the children will soon catch on and offer clever suggestions. Add

some more drama: "Let's look at the picture and think about it. How will the people know the train is coming? How can we make that sound? What will the people need to do next?" Act out the ideas. For example, move some chairs for train seating and use new words for "The wheels on the bus." Sing out! "The train on the track goes chug, chug, chug…as it takes us to our new home." Sing about the wheels going around, the train's whistle, and the conductor stamping the tickets. With a little pretending, the children can create a happy ending for the painting.

Children enjoy hearing information about the different artists and learning more about how they worked. Pablo Picasso, for example, didn't always paint the same way. He liked to try different ways to express his ideas. When he was young, he painted things just as they looked. Later, he painted mostly with pink or blue colors. When he was older, his paintings sometimes looked as if the thing he was painting was cut into pieces and shapes and pressed flat, like his painting *The Three Musicians* (Loria 1995, pp.32–3). This work has three musicians in costumes sitting behind a table. One is playing a wind instrument, one a guitar, and one is holding a sheet of music which tells us the painting is about music. "What things can you find in this painting? (Eyes, mouths, hats, instruments, tiny hands.) Where do you see the parts of a dog? Why do you think the musicians are wearing costumes?" Encourage some storytelling. "If we used colored paper and scissors and paste, we could pretend to be Picasso and make a picture like this. How could you change this picture?" Older children might also like to compare this work with Monet's painting *Waterlily Pond* discussed earlier (*The Art Book for Children, Book One*, p.69). "How are the two paintings alike? Different? Which do you like best? Why? Who has another idea?"

In addition to exploring interesting art works, add some pretending with a "frozen tableau." Georges Seurat's picturesque painting *A Sunday Afternoon on the Grande Jatte* (*The Art Book for Children, Book Two*, pp.74–5) suggests how the children might pretend to be people in a section of the painting. Older children can stage their own version of a section of the painting (a "frozen" scene or tableau) which can then be photographed by a parent or quickly sketched by interested children. Post an enlargement of the photograph so that everyone can enjoy the photographic art and sketches. Keep the

staging of the scene fairly brief and involve the children in choosing the section of the painting to portray and the roles to play. For example, the lower left of Seurat's painting has three people and a dog who is interested in their lunch, which could be staged. The interesting set of figures to the right even includes a monkey. Simple props can be made or borrowed from home, such as an umbrella, a walking stick, stuffed animals, and some imaginative hats. In addition to staging a frozen tableau, some children could create a story about it and even present it for the class. Others, after examining the reproduction up close and at a distance, might like to try to paint like Seurat using little dots of paint. Pretending to be part of a tableau can really make a work of art come alive for children.

Other paintings also lend themselves to tableaus. Ettore DeGrazia's touching and human painting *Los Ninos*, depicting children holding hands and moving together in a circle was chosen for card publication by UNICEF and has sold millions of copies worldwide. Poster copies are available through the DeGrazia Foundation (6300 North Swan, Tucson, Arizona, 857718) and would be an attractive addition to an early childhood classroom to stimulate story pretending and drama. Winslow Homer's captivating painting *Snap the Whip* (*The Art Book for Children, Book Two*, p.28) portrays a group of boys engaged in a lively recess game. Some are down and some are striving to hold the line in this engaging competition.

Still another approach to art is to explain that painters sometimes used real people as models to help them draw and paint. By selecting one of van Gogh's painting such as the one of his friend, *The Postman Roulin* (Green 2002, p.29), older children can imagine being a painter working with a real model. A child can volunteer to be the postperson and wear a cap and jacket which might be found in the dramatic play center or brought from home. A postal bag and a construction paper beard could be added along with other simple items the children might suggest. When ready, the postperson sits on a slightly higher chair so that everyone can see him and the others sit in a circle around the chair. Using a clipboard and basic art supplies, each pretend artist draws the model as they see it from their seat. Use open-ended questions to help children realize that if they are sitting behind the model, they won't be drawing the face. Even so, it is often a surprise for the group to compare drawings and realize the differences in perspective. Encourage the children to talk, dictate, or write about this experience. A similar but body view of the subject, entitled *Postman Joseph Roulin*, is available in a colorful postcard available through the Museum of Fine Arts (465 Huntington Avenue, Boston, MA 02115). Other familiar paintings can also be used in this manner to illustrate how painters worked. Models for Grant Woods's painting *American Gothic* (*The Art Book for Children, Book One*, p.42) only need a few props such as an apron, a collar, a child's plastic spade, and perhaps a pretty pin and some empty glass frames. "What kind of work do you think these people do? Why? How do you think these two people feel? Tired? Crabby? Sad? What do you see that makes you think so?" Other paintings using models might include Vermeer's mysterious *Girl with the Pearl Earring* (Bailey 1995, p.26). "What does the girl have on her head? Who do you think this girl is? What do you think she is thinking about? What do you think she is going to say?" Each work seems to suggest its own special story and many can be dramatized simply.

Another interesting way to explore paintings and stimulate thinking is to complete a picture puzzle. Make copies of a favorite painting the children have selected and cut them in half lengthwise. Each child takes a half section, tapes it to the right or left of a sheet of painting paper, and completes the painting on the other side but *in their very own way*. The results can be quite remarkable and fun to compare and talk about.

FAVORITE BOOKS ABOUT CREATING PICTURES FOR PRETENDING

Bailey, M. (1995) *Vermeer*. Ann Arbor, MI: Borders Press.

Green, J. (2002) *Vincent van Gogh*. New York, NY: Franklin Watts.

Heslewood, J. (2002) *Introducing Picasso*. North Mankato, MN: Thameside Press, distributed by Smart Apple Media.

Loria, S. (1995) *Masters of Art: Picasso*. New York, NY: Peter Bedrick Books.

Mason, A. (2002) *In the Time of Picasso*. Brookfield, CN: Copper Beech Books.

Sayre, H. (2004) *Cave Paintings to Picasso*. San Francisco, CA: Chronicle Books.*

The Art Book for Children, Book One (2005) New York, NY: Phaidon Press.*

The Art Book for Children, Book Two (2007) New York, NY: Phaidon Press.*

Venezia, M. (1988) *Getting to Know the World's Greatest Artists: Van Gogh*. Chicago, IL: Children's Press.

Welton, J. (2002) *Henri Matisse*. New York, NY: Franklin Watts.

★ These are comprehensive reference books.

Sculpture

Take advantage of children's interest and curiosity about sculpture. Potter's clay (gray, common clay) is available in bulk from ceramic stores or in powdered form from educational supply companies. If using powder, have the children help mix the powder and water to a pliable consistency, but not sticky. Kept moist and stored in a sealed plastic bag, potter's clay will remain useable for months. Clay, a little water, and a plain, plastic placemat (approximately 12×16 inches/30×40 cm) or sturdy cardboard for a base are the main materials children need for sculpting. Tongue depressors and certain kitchen utensils and tools can be used safely as sculpting tools. The play dough recipe (p.57), or commercial play dough can be used instead of potter's clay, but the clay has a special kind of feeling. Working with a flexible medium such as clay is a highly tactile experience and helps develop the sense of touch in creating art work. Items can always be reworked and, instead of a mistake, the child has a work "in progress." Clay is a true confidence builder.

Children generally begin to explore clay by pounding it with their fists, turning it over and over, or kneading it their fingers. Later they will start to name what they are making. They might shape a piece into a round ball or roll the clay to make birthday candles. Young children need introductory time to experiment with the possibilities of this medium. As they work, talk about what they are doing and ask a few probing questions. "How does the clay feel when you need to add water? How could you use your fingers to add a tiny bit of water? What else could you stick into the clay?" Older children might be challenged to sculpt a simple story character for a story box (p.109) and later use it to retell the story. As they become more adventurous, they might begin to draw, dictate, or write about their creations or demonstrate how they made them.

To stimulate creativity, look at a variety of pictures of sculptures and, if possible, visit an impressive statue nearby in the community. Children will soon realize that sculpture can be made from many different materials besides clay, including a variety of odds and ends. Enjoy together the peaceful double-page illustration of the outdoor sculpture *King and Queen* (*The Art Book for Children, Book Two*, pp.12–13) created by Henry Moore. Although the sculpture is over five feet tall and seems to command the whole countryside, it began as a little piece of wax the artist was playing with in his hands. "How do you think the king and queen feel as they look down from the hill? What do you think they are saying? How is the king's head different?" Using the inside of a large box lid, children could construct the hillside using paint, cloth, rocks, and other available materials. Then they could sculpt *their versions* of a couple to reign over the kingdom and even act out their stories.

Sayre's book (2004, p.21) has an impressive picture of a giant head carved in stone long ago by people called the Olmecs. Such large heads were portraits of Olmec rulers who wore a headpiece that almost looks like a football helmet. The statues are very big, sometimes over seven feet (two metres) tall, to remind the people how powerful their rulers were. While stone carving is not too practical, the children could locate a good-size rock and pretend to be Olmec farmers sculpting a stone head of their ruler by using paint and other interesting materials.

Another interesting sculptured stone head, *Head of a Woman*, created more recently by Picasso, is pictured in Heslewood's book (2002, Contents page, unnumbered). Although modern, there is a certain playful, almost humorous quality about the work. It certainly illustrates that the sculpture the artist created looked very different from the woman who was his model. For children, such a work can inspire experimentation and innovation.

Picasso's sculpture *The Goat*, (Heslewood 2002, p.21) is well suited for children to explore because they will be dramatizing *The Three Billy Goats Gruff*, and the sculpture provides a provocative introduction to the animal's body and bearing. While the work is majestic, one still wants to feel the animal's horn and touch its metallic fur. Children will be interested to know that Picasso used everyday things to make the goat, such as scrap iron, palm tree leaves, and a wicker basket. He then put them together with plaster and the piece was covered with bronze. Loria's book (1995, pp.50–51) contains a delightful double-page picture of Picasso working in his studio on the sculpture. It

could be challenging to pretend that you are a creative sculptor working with different materials in your studio and creating a sculpture of something that is special to you. Perhaps it might be a small piece of tree limb that suggests an image. Sometimes Picasso used everyday things such as nails, pliers, screws, and parts of a pan to make a sculpture. "What other unusual things could we use to make a sculpture? Let's do it!"

Older children appreciate *Little Dancer of Fourteen Years* by Edgar Degas (Cole and Cocca-Leffler 2001, pages in rear, unnumbered) and are surprised to hear that when Degas made this sculpture, most dancers were poor and had to work instead of going to school. Degas used a young neighbor named Marie as a model for the sculpture and made it of wax with wire inside to hold it up. Later the statue was covered in bronze. This statue is different because it is wearing real clothes and has a ribbon in the dancer's hair. Ballet dancers have to practice different body positions or poses for dancing. Examine how the girl in the statue is holding her body. Perhaps this girl is practicing a dance position or maybe she is just waiting for her turn to dance. "Look carefully and try to stand just like Marie is standing for the statue.

Now, pretend you are a different statue and pose in another position. What other ways can you hold your body?" This activity is a little like the game of "statues" or "freeze," and it's surprising how many unusual ways children can think of positioning their bodies. For more interest, add a piece of clothing or a prop.

Art and drama activities are an inviting way to involve parents in classroom events. A note home might request the family search and send items to enliven paper plate masks such as yarn, paper doilies, or buttons; a list of things needed to decorate puppets is included on p.92. Offer different ways for parents to be included in everyday art and drama activities which are adaptable to their busy schedules. Some parents might prefer to do tasks at home in the evenings while others find it convenient to visit and help individual children. An extra pair of hands is always welcome and can help parents in guiding creative thinking.

FAVORITE BOOKS ABOUT CREATING SCULPTURE FOR PRETENDING

Cole, K. and Cocca-Leffler, M. (2001) *Edgar Degas, Paintings that Dance*. New York, NY: Grosset & Dunlap (Postcards of *Little Dancer of Fourteen Years Old* are available from the Sterling and Francine Clark Institute, Williamstown, MA 01267.)

Heslewood, J. (2002) *Introducing Picasso*. North Mankato, MN: Thameside Press, distributed by Smart Apple Media.

Sayre, H. (2004) *Cave Paintings to Picasso*. San Francisco, CA: Chronicle Books.

Loria, S. (1995) *Masters of Art: Picasso*. New York, NY: Peter Bedrick Books.

The Art Book for Children, Book Two (2005) New York, NY: Phaidon Press, Inc.

Puppetry

Puppetry is yet another art form for involving young children in story pretending and drama and arousing their imagination. Puppets enable children to express their ideas and inner feelings safely, without assuming responsibility for them. After all, *they* didn't say or do that; the puppet did. Language and self-expression abound as children explore ideas and actions vicariously without fear of non-acceptance. Children with limited verbal skills or physical limitations can often use puppets to convey their ideas and allow them to take part in the action. "Look at me. I'm dancing." Using puppets, children feel less self-conscious as they explore problem solving in their own unique ways. They can test methods of working together cooperatively and experience acceptance while extending their attention span and strengthening manipulative skills.

Often teachers use a charming commercial puppet to guide the children during the daily program, and a class puppet can be warmly regarded by them and considered a friend to all. Observing the teacher modeling voice, gestures, and sounds also inspires children to try the techniques themselves. Although appealing, commercial puppets tend to be expensive, and classrooms rarely have the specific puppets needed for children to dramatize a story. Fortunately, child-created puppets provide a practical alternative, and children tend to value them because they used their ideas in creating their handiwork. While the homemade child-size puppets described in the following section may not have quite the polish of commercial ones, they are very useable and children obtain considerable satisfaction from creating them. Children also benefit from opportunities to use their puppets with others and to participate in performing and directing their own mini-dramatizations.

One of the secrets of a successful puppeteer is to *verbally interact with* the puppet. When using the class puppet, model for the children a two-way conversation that is being conducted between two participants, you and the puppet. After observing such interactions, the children will be curious to learn how to manipulate the puppet. You can explain that puppets can do a lot of things and model how the puppet can walk, run, fly, clap, wave, cry, sneeze, and go to sleep. Puppets can also indicate "yes" or "no," pick up an item, search for something, or just be shy.

Now demonstrate how to use your hand to make the puppet move. It is usually easier to begin with a simple slip-in hand puppet such as example 5 (p.90). Show the children how to place the four fingers of their dominant hand together, bend them forward a little, and then bend their thumb against the bottom of the four fingers. After practicing the position, they can practice with a slip-in puppet. To make the puppet talk, they simply bend their four fingers forward as they speak. Again, practice makes perfect.

For a puppet with two arms (6, p.91), demonstrate that you use your first three fingers (the thumb, index, and middle fingers) and fold the two remaining fingers down on the palm of the hand. Have them practice this position with the fingers of their dominant hand.

Then explain that the thumb slips into and moves the puppet's one arm, the next finger slips into and moves the puppet's head, and the last finger slips into and moves the puppet's other arm. Now it's just a matter of the children practicing with puppets individually or with a friend.

After the children have had time to enjoy manipulating the puppets, the idea of making their own puppets can sound very interesting. Children will find it both challenging and fun to make a puppet of themselves, a family member, or a favorite story character using one of the simple methods below. Puppets are more interesting if they have movement, so encourage the children to consider adding arms, legs, hair, or floppy ears, glasses, or a tail to their homemade puppet. Provide the necessary art supplies (for materials for child size puppets, see p.92), and stand back to applaud. As always, the process of creating is far more important than the final product.

To introduce the idea of children's puppets, begin with some personal, improvised pretending. You might present a story about something that happened to you, such as finding a mouse in your house, and use a homemade puppet of *yourself* to tell the tale. To make

your puppet, simply enlarge the outline for the slip-in puppet (Appendix B) to fit your hand. This can inspire the children to create personal puppets too and use them to tell, dictate, or act out their own brief personal adventures. For younger children, the teacher might narrate a story while the child's puppet speaks the dialogue. If several older children are invited to dramatize another child's story with puppets, it is usually helpful if the child who created the story is recognized as the leader. The author can assign the roles and dialogue, and the whole class can discuss the drama afterwards, offering comments and suggestions. Puppets can also use a pretend microphone to interview the audience speakers concerning their ideas.

Children can design and make a series of puppets to dramatize a familiar story from a picture book. One child can narrate the story while other children manage the dialogue and puppets. The roles can be rotated at another presentation. Puppets can also accompany songs and poems. For example, children can make their homemade animal puppets perform while the group sings "Old MacDonald had a farm." Although staging can be added, puppets need not be constrained by a stage. Puppeteers are perfectly happy using the bottom of a decorated shoebox as a stage, or sitting at either end or behind a small table, with their puppets facing the audience. This way, the puppeteers can view the action.

CHILDREN'S PUPPETS

1. Paper plate puppet

Use a 6–7-inch (15–18 cm) sturdy paper plate (Styrofoam plates are more difficult to color and can crack). Children can draw the face with magic markers or poster paint and decorate with a cork nose, pieces of ribbon, crepe paper, straws, colored pipe cleaners, etc. Attach a paint stirrer (usually available free of charge at paint stores) to the rear center of the plate with masking tape. The child manipulates the puppet by holding the bottom section of the stirrer.

2. Envelope puppet

These are not as durable but are simple and quick to make and meet the need for on-the-spot puppets. Use a heavy grade large business envelope, seal, and cut off about two inches (5 cm) along one shorter edge so that the child can slip her/his hand inside. The children decorate as above.

3. Paper roll puppet

Face puppet: For a simple version, use a 3 × 5 inch (approximately 7.5 × 12.5 cm) plain index card and an empty toilet paper roll. The child draws and decorates the face lengthwise on the card and attaches the paper roll with glue, double-sided tape, or double-folded masking tape. The card should *not* be glued around the roll but kept flat so the puppet's whole face is visible. The child can insert the index and middle fingers inside the roll to manipulate the puppet. Younger children can sit the puppet on a surface and manipulate it by holding the rear of the roll and moving it about.

Older children might prefer to decorate a face directly on the paper roll (omitting the card) and then move it from behind on a flat surface. The roll can also be decorated and used horizontally (instead of upright) to create a mouse, an angry alligator, or a scary dragon. Glue some furry cloth scraps around the tube, add a face, four cork legs, and a tail, and you have a friendly dog or cat.

Whole Body Puppet: Use a larger 5 × 8 inch (12.5 × 20 cm) plain index card, draw and decorate the whole body, and attach to a long cardboard tube. The novelty of this puppet is that it can also be manipulated *from above* by attaching a tongue depressor at the *top* of the paper roll. This enables the child to stand behind and look down to watch her/his manipulations.

4. Small box or bag puppet

Box puppet: Use an individual-size cereal box and tape the top shut. Make a hole near the top rear of the box to snugly allow the child to insert her/his index or middle finger to manipulate the puppet. Paint with poster paint, or tape construction paper around the box and decorate the front section and top for the puppet face. Arms and legs can be cut from paper and pasted to the sides and bottom if desired.

Bag puppet: Stuff half of a paper bag (size 5 works well) with crumpled newspaper and tie securely in the middle with string. Twist the lower half of the bag to form a handle to hold the puppet. The child decorates the upper half for the face.

5. Child-size slip-in hand puppet

This requires a little preparation but is more durable, and the child can create a soft puppet with a great deal of versatility. Ask a parent to trace around the outline for a slip-in hand puppet (Appendix B), and cut two pattern pieces from felt material. Simply glue the edges together with craft glue (available at craft stores), leaving the bottom open for the child's hand to slip inside. Edges can also be fastened by an adult sewing them or using a glue gun. These do not need to be turned inside as felt does not fray.

Permanent face: The child can use poster paint directly on the felt to create a face and add yarn hair and other desired odds and ends for decoration.

Changeable face: The child draws and decorates a face on a circle 3 inches in diameter, cut from a 3 × 5 inch (7.5 × 12.5 cm) index card. The top of the face is then fastened to the top of the puppet with double-sided tape or a small-size office pinch clip. The face can then be removed and another face applied.

Sock puppet variation: For a very simple slip-in hand puppet, use a small-size white ankle sock with a smooth surface. Lay it flat with the heel section to the rear, and the children can decorate the front.

6. Child-size hand puppet with arms

This is similar to the above puppet but a bit more challenging to manipulate. Trace around the easy-to-sew outline for a hand puppet with arms (Appendix B), and cut two pattern pieces from felt or other non-fraying material. Ask a parent to sew around the edges or glue the edges with craft glue, leaving the bottom edge open for the child's hand to slip inside. The child can use poster paints and other odds and ends to create a face directly on the felt. Model how the thumb is used to move one arm, the index finger to move the head, and the middle finger to move the other arm. To make a puppet face that can be changed, see 5, Changeable face, above.

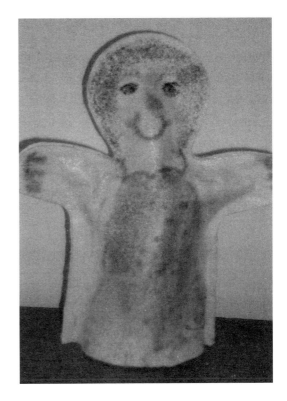

Figure 4.1: Child-size slip-in hand puppet

ART MATERIALS FOR CHILD-SIZE PUPPETS:

- General: construction paper, scissors, felt markers, poster paint and brushes, Scotch® tape (single- and double-sided), Sobo® or similar glue.

- Specific: Puppet 1: Paper plate, (6 or 7 inch/15 or 18 cm round), paint stirrer

  Puppet 2: Large business envelope

  Puppet 3: Empty toilet or kitchen roll

  3 × 5 inch (7.5 × 12.5 cm) or 5 × 8 inch (12.5 × 20 cm) index cards

  Puppet 4: Individual-size cereal box or size 5 paper bag

  Puppet 5: Felt or other non-fraying material or child-size white ankle sock

  Puppet 6: Felt or non-fraying material.

- Decorative: Ribbon, crepe paper, yarn, cotton balls, corks, straws, colored pipe cleaners, feathers, buttons, scraps of furry and other fabrics, rick rack, lace, aluminum foil, craft sticks, pompoms, and old "jewels."

DRAMA AND MUSIC

Songs and instruments

Children are drawn to the rhythmic patterns of songs and, by listening and singing, develop an interest in recognizing sounds and playing with words. The words of a song often convey a storyline which can help in developing comprehension skills. Songs and melodies are also useful in accompanying and extending dramatizations and, when combined with body movements, provide relaxation and enjoyment. Children benefit when music is part of their day.

When using songs, introduce ones that allow children to sing and do actions at the same time. This adds an appealing dimension. Choose simple songs with a strong, rhythmic melody, only a few lines, and easy words to learn. Songs such as "Where is Thumbkin?" "The wheels on the bus," "If you're happy and you know it," and "The bear went over the mountain" (found in the book list at the end of this section) offer action and are good starters. Young children especially like singing about animals, holidays, and themselves. Just watch their faces light up when their name, clothing, or experiences are inserted in a song. Their singing range is between middle C and C or D above middle C and songs will need to be lowered if they are pitched too high.

Simply gather the children together (no toys, please) and sing the song several times, and as the melody and words become familiar, invite the children to join in. Introduce several songs a week and soon the children will have a basic collection for group singing time. Younger children like to listen at first and may only sing a word or two, but momentum is gained as they have more experience. Lead the way and model being completely involved in the singing, joining the actions, using facial expressions, and sharing your enthusiasm. Singing quality is unimportant as the emphasis is in the joy of singing together. Include songs that are representative of the cultures of the group, and invite parents to introduce these special songs to the children. Songs can be accompanied by a large tambourine or rhythm drum, and autoharp and guitar chording is

available for a number of traditional children's songs (Isbell and Raines 2007).

When the children are comfortable singing together, play around with a few words in a familiar song and add some drama. The old favorite "Did you ever see a lassie?" can be changed to include zoo animals and adding actions which the children suggest and *discuss*.

Did You Ever See a Lassie?

Did you ever see the alligator,
the alligator, the alligator,
go this way and that way?
Did you ever see the alligator
that lives at the zoo?

The children might put their hands together and stretch out their arms to create a snapping alligator, and close their eyes to pretend the alligator is sleeping in the murky water. What about pretending a puppy, a snake, a tiger, or a fireman?

Give children the opportunity to hear and join others in the joy of singing. You might arrange for one or two members from the school chorus, community glee club, or a barber shop quartet to sing a few old favorites, and then have the children join the singing. What about a sing-along with a talented parent? A number of picture songbooks use the texts from favorite songs and provide humor and often attractive illustrations to practice picture reading. Class volunteers can dramatize different parts of the song as the others sing the words. Older children like to use song flipcharts with the teacher pointing to the words as they sing. By using picture songbooks or picture/word charts, emergent readers can actively connect the spoken word with the written word and gain confidence in their reading ability.

FAVORITE SONGBOOKS FOR PRETENDING

Berry, H. (1994) *Old MacDonald had a Farm*. New York, NY: North-South Books.

Bullock, K. (1993) *She'll be Comin' Round the Mountain*. New York, NY: Simon and Schuster.

Isbell, R. and Raines, S. (2007) *Creativity and the Arts with Young Children*. Clifton Park: Thomson-Delmar Learning.

Kidd, R. (1992) *On Top of Old Smoky: A Collection of Songs and Stories from Appalachia*. Nashville, TN: Ideals Children's Books.

Kovalski, M. (1990) *The Wheels on the Bus: An Adaption of the Traditional Song*. New York, NY: Little, Brown.

Orozco, J. (1994) *De Colores and Other Latin-American Folk Songs for Children*. New York, NY: Dutton Children's Books.

Peek, M. (1981) *Roll Over! A Counting Song*. New York, NY: Houghton Mifflin.

FAVORITE SONG RECORDINGS FOR PRETENDING

Jenkins, E. (1992) *You'll Sing a Song and I'll Sing a Song*. Washington, DC: Smithsonian Folkways Recordings.

Jenkins, E. (1995) *Multicultural Children's Songs*. Washington, DC: Smithsonian Folkways Recordings.

Raffi (1996) *Rise and Shine*. Cambridge, MA: Rounder Records.

Just listening is another important and enjoyable aspect of music. During the day, play sections of different background music to accompany various activities. Children generally enjoy all kinds of music, from the classics to jazz, so music can easily be matched to the mood of an activity. Notice opportunities to point out differences between music such as classical, folk, cowboy, Native American, jazz, African, oriental, and marching. Ask, "How do you feel when you hear this music? How does it make you want to move? Show us." Older children enjoy listening to the recording of Sergei Prokofiev's *Peter and the Wolf*, narrated by Boris Karloff (1957), which combines storytelling and music to expand a good tale. Talk about how the music patterns signal when Peter is walking along or the wolf is about to enter, and act out a section or two. Sometimes children can suggest a melody to accompany a section of a favorite picture book being reread. Take advantage, too, of a brief time block to have the children really concentrate and listen to a specific selection of music. Remember their limited attention span and keep the piece under three or four minutes. Try some innovation. Adapt and tell older children the story of Tchaikovsky's *Swan Lake* (Karirer 2004). Invite a young ballet student or local teacher to visit and demonstrate some basic positions or perform a section of the music from the ballet. Such experiences can create a pretend environment which children can enter by closing their eyes, swaying, sketching, or just watching and appreciating.

Instruments can be combined with singing and listening and are another way to enhance pretending. Provide an out-of-the-way spot in the room where children can individually explore musical instruments and their sounds, *a few instruments at a time*. Wrist bells and rhythm sticks blend well to start, and sand blocks, triangles, maracas, drums and tambourines can be added gradually. Children need guidance to explore the instruments appropriately and to experiment with the sounds and using rhythm patterns. A musical parent might enjoy helping in this way. A parent musician might also be invited to perform for the children and afterwards help them use the instrument appropriately and even create some interesting sounds. Ask around. Perhaps a member of the high school band or community orchestra would also enjoy playing for the children. If the musician is a drummer, the children might pretend a "jam session" by accompanying the drums with kazoos. A class volunteer could pretend to be the conductor.

Encourage children to hear and create random sound effects in the environment. Paper can be crumbled to sound like a roaring fire, water can be squeezed from a sponge to sound like a stream, and taping wooden unit blocks can indicate walking steps. A cymbal can represent an effective crash by using one side of the cymbal and a padded homemade mallet.

Use sounds to accompany chanting, singing, and movements, and especially to add excitement to story pretending and drama. Two groups with different sets of instruments can alternately accompany singing, guided by a volunteer conductor.

Imagine the fun of planning and using sound effects to accompany a dramatization of Sendak's book (1963) *Where the Wild Things Are* (see p.77), or using a hand slap on the drum as a goat goes across the bridge in our storybook. Special sound effects can certainly capture the attention of the audience. When a repetitive phrase is chanted, the audience can emphasize the words with instruments or other sounds such as clapping, tapping fingers on the floor, or the delightful sound of humming. Children can also select an instrument to represent a certain story character to enliven a retelling. The following recordings provide lovely music for listening, moving, and dramatizing.

FAVORITE LISTENING RECORDINGS FOR PRETENDING

Fidler, A. (1993) *Classics or Kids*. New York, NY: RCA Victor.

Prokofiev, S. (1957) *Peter and the Wolf*. New York, NY: Vanguard Classics.

Tchaikovsky, P. (2004) *Swan Lake*. London: EMI Classics. Accompanying Storybook: Karirer, K. (2004) *Swan Lake*. New York, NY: Golden Books.

Various composers (2000) *Good Music for Little Guys: Classics for Fun and Adventure*. Hollywood, CA: Delos International.

Zane, D. (2000) *76 Trombones and other Broadway Standards*. New York, NY: Little Life Studio/Playback Studio.

Movement and yoga

Young children are natural movers and doers. They run, jump, twirl, and pretend in uninhibited ways, expressing a variety of inward feelings while exercising their bodies. Movement is necessary to increase their agility, mobility, and coordination and to provide needed release from periods of inactivity. In addition, children's vocabulary is enhanced by actually experiencing the meaning of words associated with dramatic movements. Body parts such as elbows, ankles, wrists, and knees, and challenging terms such as right/left, wide/narrow, inside/outside, and in front/behind acquire meaning through actual use. Words describing facial gestures such as frowning, pursing your lips, and narrowing your eyes can also be experienced in drama. Fortunately, young children can be refreshed by movement breaks and motivated to imagine, pretend, refocus, and concentrate.

While some children are quite spontaneous in expressing themselves in movement, others are more hesitant and self-conscious, especially when being observed. For most children, the ability to express themselves through movement evolves *gradually*, and therefore using movement in the classroom needs to progress gradually from *simple* experiences to more *complex* ones with adequate reinforcement along the way. Set the stage by briefly talking about how important it is to use your body. Usually, the word "movement" tends to arouse more interest than the word "dance." Discuss that basketball players, ice skaters, and other athletes learn about movement so they can control their bodies and move easily. Emphasize there is no one right way to move. Each person's body is different, but everyone can learn to do more with their body by using it. Then slowly introduce a few basic stretches to do together. "Stretch up high; clasp your hands; bend to the right (windows) and to the left (door); now slowly bend at the waist and just 'hang;' then slowly raise your body." Such beginning movements can be used whenever children obviously need a "time out." Older children can volunteer to lead the group while others offer their own ideas.

Arrange for sufficient space and establish safety guidelines such as moving in one direction so no one is hurt and using a stopping signal (e.g. a raised arm, a drum tap). Additional movements can be introduced during a group circle time. Previous to this, notice during the morning when a child is doing a spontaneous basic movement such as twirling, hopping, or jumping, and comment, "What a neat way you're moving," or

"You're really having fun moving." You might offer to clap, sing, or tap a tambourine to follow the child's movement. Then, at circle time, ask the child, "Lydia, can you show us how you were moving this morning?" The child will usually be happy to model, and others can join the fun. Usually, the next question is, "Who knows another way to move?" and other suggestions such a walking on tiptoe or running in place can be explored. As movement is voluntary, cautious children are comfortable just watching.

Movements can be extended by pretending to play a drum while marching or catching a basketball after shooting a basket. Moving to a favorite selection of music is more fun if something is moving with you, and simple props such as small scarves or bracelet bells can be added. Children can also make movement wands by decorating a sturdy paper towel holder and cutting five strips of bright crepe paper about 25 inches (65 cm) long. The tops of the strips are folded together and stapled to the top of the holder. (A parent can guide the children in the measuring, cutting, and stapling.) When not in use, the strips can be rolled around the holder and stored in a box. Such group activities let children explore movement at their own pace without feeling self-conscious. Their movements reflect their own innovative ideas which are noted and respected, and this further instills confidence.

When the children are comfortable using movements, add some mini-drama. They might narrate and pretend having a picnic and it suddenly rains. Add instruments, tapping a drum for thunder and striking rhythm sticks for the raindrops. Body movements such as opening an umbrella or collecting picnic items can indicate the change in weather. Create movements to accompany parts of a favorite story such as Beatrix Potter's *Peter Rabbit*: "How can we move to pretend we're Peter in the watering can, or trying to avoid the white cat? Who knows another way?" Provide opportunities to draw, dictate, or write about their pretending. Such activities may last only a few minutes but are invaluable when children need to enter a pretend world to think and relax.

FAVORITE MOVEMENT BOOKS FOR PRETENDING

Cauley, L. (1997) *Clap your Hands*. New York, NY: Puffin.
Jenkins, S. (2006) *Move!* New York, NY: Houghton Mifflin.
Ormerod, J. (2011) *Whoosh Around the Mulberrry Bush*. Hauppauge, NY: Barrones Educational Series.
Williams, L. (1988) *The Little Old Lady Who Wasn't Afraid of Anything*. New York, NY: HarperCollins.

Integrate yoga into story pretending and drama. Introduce some of the basic yoga positions which represent things children recognize such as the tree, bird, dog, cat, frog, cobra, fish, and lion. Later suitable positions include the mountain, rocking horse, woodchopper, and stork, among others. When introducing children's yoga, the book *Be a Frog, a Bird, or a Tree* by Rachael Carr (1973) is a valuable resource for teachers and children because the large illustrations feature children doing the movements. Unfortunately, the work is no longer in print but copies are available on the internet.

Use a circle arrangement so everyone can see, and try to have no more than six to eight children in a beginning group. The rest of the group could be involved in other activities, or perhaps an interested parent or aide could work with a second group if space permits. Or do yoga with several small groups at different times. Keep the sessions brief, about three to five minutes. Children's yoga is quite casual and especially enjoyable in bare feet.

Children should be encouraged to do only what feels comfortable, which means *their version of a movement*. For example, in pretending to be a tree, one child might place a foot on the opposite leg while another prefers to be a firm tree with both feet on the ground. Introduce one or two movements at a time. Hold a position briefly and then encourage the children to improvise by pretending variations. There is no rule that says a yoga position cannot move and change! "How can your tree move in a gentle breeze? or a strong wind? Can your tree have a bird nest in its leaves? Can your frog hop on the rocks in a pretend stream?" Using a nature or outdoor theme, the children might invent a yoga movement for a rainbow, a cloud, or a wilting flower. Eventually, they can build a repertoire of *their* yoga-based movements. Such movements can be used to act out parts of a picture book story, a poem, or rhyme, or to create new positions to accompany story retellings. Working together, the children learn from each other and can help each other when coaching is needed.

FAVORITE YOGA BOOKS FOR PRETENDING

Carr, R. (1973) *Be a Frog, a Bird, or a Tree*. Garden City, New York, NY: Doubleday. (Out of print; available on the internet.)

Guber, T. and Kalish, L. (2005) *Yoga Pretzels*. Cambridge, MA: Barefoot Books.

Power, T. (2009) *The ABCs of Yoga for Kids*. Wellington, New Zealand: Stafford House.

Stewart, M. (1992) *Yoga for Children*. New York, NY: Simon and Schuster.

Chapter 5

ACTION: GETTING READY FOR STORY DRAMATIZATION

LEARNING THE STORY

After children have had experience in using dramatic play and everyday daily drama activities, many will be ready and interested in dramatizing the story *The Three Billy Goats Gruff*, presented in Part 3. Other younger children might not yet be ready and will be content to continue current dramatic undertakings.

To dramatize a story, children need to know it thoroughly, and hearing it retold in different ways is an appealing method of learning it. While there are many ways to help children learn a story, the sequential approach of, first, telling the story, second, reading the storybook, and, third, picture-reading the storybook, firmly implants the narrative in the child's mind and imagination. Each retelling repeats the pattern of events, and using different approaches captures the children's attention. The number of retellings, however, depends on the children's needs and can vary from group to group. The goal is to have the children learn the story, and the teacher plans accordingly. Even teachers who do not consider themselves particularly "dramatic" will find this sequential approach to learning *The Three Billy Goats Gruff* to be a flexible and workable way to prepare for its dramatization.

A good time to begin informal story dramatization is usually towards the middle of the year. Not only are children more comfortable pretending, but they have also had time to adjust to the class routine and to develop effective ways of interacting in a group. Often at this time of the year, the weather is harsh, and children who are confined indoors can be restless and eager for action. During these colder months, they seem especially open to new and challenging activities, and story dramatization certainly offers an attractive response.

Tell the story

Storytelling has been an engaging experience for young children for centuries and is a supportive first step in introducing a story for dramatization. Without the help of a book, children must rely on their imagination to create the setting, the characters, and the action, and think about the story to understand how the events connect sequentially. Through the storyteller's skill, they come face to face with the characters and imagine feelings they may have also experienced. New vocabulary can be expanded within the context, and casual clues can be inserted to suggest alternative story ideas. Effective storytelling is indeed a personal experience which lures children into the web of a story and helps prepare them to portray it.

Telling is more leisurely for the storyteller too, as there are no concerns about print to follow, pages to turn, or whether everyone can see the book. The teacher merely acts out the story, communicating directly with the audience and using a variety of techniques that add meaning and aid comprehension. Not being bound by a book, the storyteller can "read" the audience and pause when there is a hint of confusion or a question that obviously requires attention. Generally, the initial storytelling is mainly for listening and to familiarize the children with the tale. They will become more involved in subsequent retellings.

A captivating storyteller begins with a story that is "just right" because it corresponds with the interests of the audience. *The Three Billy Goats Gruff* is well suited for both telling and story dramatization because it contains characteristics that appeal to young children:

- a well-structured plot with a beginning, middle, and end, often with a problem and an element of surprise

- a predictable, repetitive storyline that involves action and accompanying sounds and gestures

- colorful, active characters who use simple, direct dialogue that can be easily followed, understood, and remembered

- rhythmic language with repeated phrases and humorous, rhyming words

- a lesson or moral that adds meaning to the story.

Although the book uses *The Three Billy Goats Gruff* as the beginning tale to dramatize, additional stories for dramatization are listed on p.76.

To prepare to tell *The Three Billy Goats Gruff*, read the picture storybook version and think about the possible setting, what the characters might look like, how the plot evolves event by event, and the excitement of the action. Consider the possible facial gestures and movements of the characters as your modeling motivates the children to imitate and create their own interpretations. Then casually tell the story to yourself in your own words. Next, try telling the story in front of a mirror and experiment with different mannerisms, not too exaggerated but enough to hold the attention of the children. When using dialogue, say the words as if you're actually speaking them to someone. Vary your pacing, sometimes talking quickly and at other times more slowly. Match your tone to the mood of the plot, using a louder voice for action and a softer one for suspense. Vary the pitch of your voice. Try a high, baby voice for Billy Goat One and a deep, grumpy voice for the Troll. Convey emotion and accompany your words with actions when needed. Shake your fist, point your finger. Raise your eyebrows, widen your eyes, and raise your hands to indicate surprise. You might pause or be silent at times, but always use techniques with which you are comfortable. If all this seems a bit challenging, you might borrow a DVD from the library and observe a skilled children's storyteller in action. When you feel confident, try telling the story to a supportive friend and ask for feedback. For a thoroughly genuine reaction, tell it to several young children.

To tell the story to the class, have the children sit in a semicircle, allowing a hand of space between them. It is helpful to have a large "X" in each spot to designate a *home* base for each child to sit. It is also useful later after a story dramatization when the audience returns to their circle spots for the follow-up discussion. Agree on a sign (e.g. two fingers over your mouth) to indicate a storytelling, or announce in an animated voice, "Time to listen. I'm going to tell a story." At a later time, when you feel really adventurous, you might create a special dramatic atmosphere by lowering the blinds a bit, piling a few tree limbs in the center of the circle, adding some crumpled red cellophane, and tell the tale gathered around a pretend campfire.

Telling a story is often a new and novel approach, so begin by explaining that the story will be told without using a picture book and that they will have to listen carefully and use their imagination to "see" the story in their heads. The focus is now on listening and a simple overview provides a useful introduction; "This story is about a mean troll who got into a lot of trouble because he didn't know how to share." Having aroused their curiosity, try a question that relates the story to their own experiences. "What are some of the things we share? How do you feel when someone doesn't share with you?"

When introducing the story, emphasize special features that will help the children visualize a character, such as the Troll's long nose and squinty, sharp eyes.

Now, assume a secretive approach and begin the storytelling. Punctuate the story with several words or phrases that have special appeal and arouse interest such as "surprise," "different," "maybe," and "guess what?" As you speak, maintain eye contact and watch the children's expressions for interest, confusion, or distraction, and be ready to respond accordingly. Above all, be involved in the story!

Plan to close the storytelling with some thought-provoking comments and questions to stimulate an exchange of ideas. This not only makes responding and feedback a habit, but it also cultivates a more natural balance of speech between the teacher and the group. Being in a circle, the children can see and gauge the reactions of others while open-ended questions stimulate conversation. "What part did you like best about the story? Which character was your favorite? Why? Can you think of a better way to solve the problem?" A question such as "How did I show Billy Goat One was frightened when I was telling the story?" spotlights your use of dramatic techniques. Model ways of introducing their ideas such as "I think that…," or "I have another idea. We could…," or "What about…?" When a child strays off topic, the teacher can gently remind, "We're only talking about the story right now. We can talk about that later." Reminding the group of class rules, such as "Wait until a friend stops talking before you start talking," provides listening practice and encourages sensitivity to the feelings of others. Sometimes a discussion can take an unexpected turn because of different experiences or cultural backgrounds, and the teacher can use the situation to foster understanding. "Some people lower their eyes when they answer to show they are respectful." Overall, the sharing time following storytelling is especially valuable because it enables children to practice listening, speaking, and thinking in a relaxed and accepting atmosphere.

Read and picture-read the story

For the next retelling, introduce the picture book version of the story to the children. Younger children may be surprised to see that a story they recently heard is written in a book. As they are already familiar with the plot, this reading can be more casual and focus on involving the children in the story. As you read the text, volunteers can be encouraged to add missing words, contribute dialogue and impromptu lines, chorus a repetitive phrase, or even provide some sound effects. This reading not only reviews the story but offers children an opportunity to become part of it and *make it their own*. By tying illustrations to the story, the reading also provides a prelude to picture-reading the book, an important next step.

Surprisingly, the opportunity for children to picture-read books is often overlooked. Adults may occasionally point to picture details when reading a story, but children are rarely encouraged to assume the task of later "reading" the pictures themselves. Sulzby (1985) outlines the child's natural progression of moving from pointing and labeling pictures, to picture reading, to using book language in telling the story, and, finally, to reading the text. Obviously, picture reading is a valuable reading skill which gradually links the oral story to the printed text. As children begin to connect the pictures and words in the text, they also gain confidence and sense that they can "read" the story.

While the text and pictures in most children's picture books are equally important, some book illustrations are primary and especially helpful in guiding non-readers in retelling the story. Such books illustrate the sequence of events page by page, highlight the action without distracting details, and indicate the repetitious flow of the words in the story. Children can easily scan them, left to right, looking for clues about the storyline to determine what is happening. The simplicity of fables, wordless and predictable books, and such universal favorites as Slobodkina's *Caps for Sale* (1940) (see p.77), and Cowley's *Mrs.Wishy-Washy* (1980) (see p.76) lend themselves to picture reading. Many different types of pictures, such as photographs, line drawings, or collages, can be used effectively in picture reading. The storybook for *The Three Billy Goats Gruff* (Chapter 6) was designed for beginning picture reading and uses simple, silhouette illustrations. This may be downloaded and copies made so that children can picture-read with friends (see www.jkp.com).

After reading the picture storybook to the children, explain that because they know the story, they can tell what is happening by looking carefully at the pictures. "What do you think is happening in this picture? How did you know that was Billy Goat Three?" Children can also be encouraged to look for picture clues by asking, "Did you notice…? What do you think this could mean? What's happening over here?"

After reviewing the illustrations, challenge the children to retell the story by picture-reading it: "Now it's your turn to tell the story by reading the pictures in the book." The class can retell the story together or volunteers can take turns telling the story page by page. Some might volunteer to hold the book or turn the pages. The children's picture retelling usually follows the familiar storyline, but be prepared for some impromptu twists and turns. At the end, be sure to acknowledge their efforts: "Wow! You all did a great job of reading the pictures and telling the story. You are beginning to read!"

As a follow-up activity, download and print copies of the storybook so that friends can take turns picture reading during spare moments (Figure 5.1).

Place copies of the storybook in the class library to picture-read to a favorite stuffed animal. Copies can also be taken home so the children can picture-read for parents. Include a brief reminder to parents that picture reading is an important pre-reading skill that can be practiced at home. Some children might even visit another classroom to picture-read to others. Often children enjoy hearing themselves on tape and a parent could record picture readings and place copies in the listening area.

Figure 5.1: Using the storybook

OPTIONAL RETELLINGS
Flannelboards

Once children have learned a story, they are often delighted to tell it to others. Using a flannelboard or using a story box are particularly effective ways to do this because both are enjoyable and easy for children to manage. The items used can also provide clues concerning the sequence of story events.

When using a flannelboard, the storyteller simply adheres pictures of story items to a flannel-covered board as the story is being told (Figure 5.2).

A flannelboard is used as an optional retelling method when dramatizing *The Three Billy Goats Gruff* in Part 3. Suggestions for using the flannelboard, along with story pictures and directions for mounting them, are provided in the performing guide for this story in Chapter 6.

Some classrooms already have a flannelboard, but if yours does not, the following folding flannelboard is simple to make, inexpensive, and easy to store. It can also be an interesting task for a handy parent.

How to make a folding flannelboard

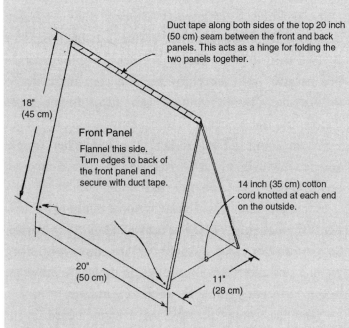

Duct tape along both sides of the top 20 inch (50 cm) seam between the front and back panels. This acts as a hinge for folding the two panels together.

18" (45 cm)

Front Panel

Flannel this side. Turn edges to back of the front panel and secure with duct tape.

14 inch (35 cm) cotton cord knotted at each end on the outside.

20" (50 cm)

11" (28 cm)

1. Obtain a large, sturdy cardboard box and cut two sections approximately 18 × 20 inches (45 × 50 cm) each.

2. Cut a piece of flannel cloth 19 × 21 inches (48 × 53 cm). White, light blue, or black flannel provide good backgrounds. Felt cloth can also be used and provides a durable surface but is more expensive.

3. Spray one cardboard section *lightly* with spray adhesive and wait one minute. Then lay the flannel on the sprayed surface, allowing a one-inch (2.5 cm) overlap all around the cardboard. Smooth gently.

4. Fold the overlap to the back of the cardboard and fasten with two-inch duct tape or heavy duty shipping tape.

5. Attach the two 20-inch (50 cm) edges by running tape over the length of the connecting seam on both the top and bottom. This seam will act as a hinge for folding the two panels together with the cloth surface to the outside.

6. Punch two holes opposite each other at each of the bottom corners of the two cardboard pieces. To finish one side, cut a piece of sturdy twine 14 inches (35 cm) long and double-knot one end. Thread the unknotted end of twine from one hole (in the front) through the opposite hole (in the back) and double-knot the end. There will be a knot on the outside of both the front and back pieces. Finish the other side the same way... and you have a great flannelboard!

Figure 5.2: Telling a flannelboard story

Story boxes

Using a story box is another way to involve children in retelling stories (Figure 5.3). They simply remove miniature objects representing story characters or items from a box as they retell the story. Children enjoy the novelty, the element of surprise, and that *they* are managing the storytelling. A study shoebox which can be decorated is an adequate container, and miniatures can be made by the children or found at dollar or craft stores. The children can be quite original in creating miniatures. Homemade dough (p.57), can be shaped, dried, and painted to represent story characters and objects. A list can also be sent to parents requesting needed items so that an extra story box can be available for the children to take home and do a retelling for the family.

Once the basic items are gathered, the teacher can model using the objects to act out the story by removing them sequentially from the box. After observing the modeling, individual volunteers can use the objects to tell the story or pairs of children can rotate telling the story to each other.

Figure 5.3: Girl using story box materials

To encourage speech, friendships, and English language learners, you might encourage or pair a less fluent speaker to work with a congenial, fluent speaker. Providing a plain colored plastic placemat to serve as the "stage" surface keeps the materials in one place, and a quiet spot ensures that the children can hear each other. Some teachers adopt the rule that children using the story boxes cannot be disturbed.

An attraction of story boxes is that they can be used for other pretending as well as for learning a story to dramatize. Initially, very young children can begin pretending by using familiar items such as a few miniature (but not too small) plastic family figures and household objects. The items can be placed inside the lid of a sturdy box used to ship mimeograph (printer) paper, and played with individually or with a friend. Children will often spend considerable time just manipulating the items before pretending. The open box lid rather resembles a horizontal one-room dollhouse, and the lid and contents can easily be returned to a storage shelf. Another box might contain small trucks, construction vehicles, and some community figures. Children might draw roads inside the box top and use language to label and describe the action as well as tell a story.

Older children can use story boxes in conjunction with a class theme they are studying, such as sea life. The children can make or collect miniature sea creatures for the box and create their own adventure stories to pretend and dramatize with the figures. Children can also select a favorite story, song, or poem, and plan the story box items needed to act out a story.

PLANNING AND INVOLVING THE CHILDREN

Having learned the story through the retellings, the children should have a firm grasp of the plot and characters. Now is a good time to introduce the idea of "acting out" the story and start planning the first dramatization, *The Three Billy Goats Gruff* (Chapter 6).

Involving the children in planning is a key feature of story dramatization. As children contribute to creative thinking, problem solving, and decision making, the drama becomes *their* undertaking and they feel more competent about their efforts. Being a planner not only expands their grasp of the story but broadens their view of dramatization to include new ideas and vocabulary such as performers, stage hands, prop managers, prompters, and sound effects. In many ways, young planners begin to *think theater*.

Staging

Begin by creating the "atmosphere" of the story in the minds of the children. After hearing the retellings, you might ask them to close their eyes and pretend they are one of the billy goats in the story. "What things do you see?" A rocky hillside, a bridge, an angry-looking troll, and another hill with delicious grass to eat? When they open their eyes and look around the classroom, they can talk about the things they imagined. "What other animals could live in the hills? Where would be a good place for the Troll to hide? What does the delicious grass look like? Does someone have a different idea?"

Talk about needing a space large enough to act out the story and encourage the children to make suggestions and be decision makers. Often an area used for group gatherings such as the reading area is adaptable. Consider what can be moved or removed, even temporarily, to provide additional space. Where could the audience sit? Is there an area with a cozy rug where children can sit in a semicircular arrangement, allowing everyone to see the action? Think outside the classroom. Can the dramatization be performed in a larger meeting room, outside on the lawn, or even on the playground? What about the gym?

After the dramatization area is decided, consider the stage space. What props are needed? Where can the stage be placed? Where can the performers enter and leave the stage? Where can the chorus stand? Spatial reasoning is involved, and a number of possibilities may be offered. Accept all ideas and try different suggestions. Some decisions might best be solved by voting. To simplify the counting, the children can merely stand in a line and the "yes" votes step forward. When final decisions are made, older children might like to chalk the floor to indicate the placement of essential props.

Related considerations can also stimulate ideas. "How can we make our room look more like a theater? What kind of sign would say that this is a place to pretend stories? How will the audience know when to clap or applaud?" Contributing solutions can provide sound experience in sharing and respecting the ideas of others.

Ways to participate

Children can usually decide how they want to participate in a story drama when they understand the choices and what they involve. You might begin by introducing the idea of pretending to be a character in a story and what that means. For example, when playing the role of the Troll, you need to talk and act like the Troll. You need to *be* the Troll. Let them ponder: "What character would you like to be?" While this may sound exciting to some, children also need to realize that there are other appealing ways to participate: "What other kinds of jobs are needed in our play?" Consider the people who set up the stage, take care of the costumes and props, are part of the chorus and audience, or make the sound effects: Children can also participate by being on stage in non-speaking ways. They can add atmosphere by having a picture sign and pretending to be a bird, a tree, or a section of grass, or being a "walk on" with a sign indicating "Time to clap." For less outgoing children or English language learners, participating in this way provides an opportunity to be included without feeling in the spotlight. As their confidence grows, so can their involvement. If a final performance is planned for others, there are even more tasks such as making invitations or planning and serving simple refreshments. Conversations about ways to participate need not be time-consuming, but occur as brief time slots arise. This gives the children time to think about the options and choose a comfortable starting level of participation.

When the children are familiar with the choices, consider how to arrange individual assignments. You might, for example, draw name cards and have each child choose a role or a task for a practice time. It's surprising how quickly children can recognize the names of classmates when drama assignments are involved. When all the roles and tasks are selected, the remaining children will be the audience, with the guarantee that their names will be drawn *first* for the next practice. Although children will not always obtain exactly the assignment they want, by rotating assignments in some manner, they will be able to explore a variety of means of participating.

Props and costumes

Just asking, "What do we need for our play?" sparks children's interest and helps them to further visualize the story and the action. You might start with the stage and offer an idea such as creating a background by painting several large boxes to look like hills. "Now, who has another idea?" Keep the ideas flowing by adding some prompting questions. "Can we turn the rocking boat upside down and use it for a bridge? How could we make some grass for the billy goats?" Involving children in making and finding props is far more challenging than having them provided by others. Even if the children's suggestions are not always practical, the process is stimulating and they are thinking innovatively and expressing ideas.

Review the list of characters and ask what things could help the children look and feel like a certain story character. Even the hint of a costume is important for young children as it helps transform them into the identity of the character. Generally, simple and durable props and costumes are best, with an emphasis on durable. A homemade paper-plate mask attached to a paint stirrer is enough to turn a young child into a performer. This type of mask also has the advantage of being held away from the face so that the child does not feel confined. Even a little face paint applied by a parent volunteer can create a fierce dog or a friendly mouse. A colorful scarf, a jaunty hat, sunglasses, and the like can accomplish a pretend transformation. Props and costumes, however, need to be minimal and easy to manage so they aren't distracting.

Talk about ways to manage and organize the different assignments involved in dramatizing, such as providing sound effects and managing the props: "How can we make the sound of goats on the bridge? Where can we keep the props?" If the children are temporarily stumped, be prepared with a suggestion, such as pasting a card drawing on the prop box to show what is inside. The children can also ask or dictate a note to the office staff to save empty boxes from paper shipments to store props and costumes.

An occasional note or email can keep parents advised as to drama plans so they know what specific items are needed and how they can help. Try to include a number of ways for them to volunteer which accommodate their schedules. Does the narrator need a pretend microphone? A parent and child can find an old tennis ball at home and glue it to the top of a paper towel holder to create the needed prop. Even busy parents or a grandparent might visit for an hour to help the children make masks or cut and paste pretend grass.

The performance guide for *The Three Billy Goats Gruff* (Chapter 6) contains staging suggestions and a list of basic props and costumes, but these are always optional and adaptable. If a chorus is used, consider including bells and rhythm sticks or a tambourine or drum to accompany chanting. A child might volunteer to be the conductor when there is chanting. If older children are giving a final performance for others, you might add posters, invitations, and even a simple program listing *all the participants*, including the audience. Again, guide the children to think, talk, and be creative!

Practicing

Practicing a story opens a whole new area of pretending to children. Begin by introducing the word "practice" or "tryout" as a chance to *try different ways* to pretend a story. Explain that if one way doesn't work, we can just stop and try different words or actions to tell the story. When we are pleased with our story acting, we can have a *special* story pretending called a *performance*. We could even invite friends to see it. (Actually, there could be several performances so that the children can experience rotating roles and tasks.)

To have a beginning practice or tryout, the teacher narrates the storybook and selected characters speak the dialogue which is generally remembered from the storybook. However, other exciting things are happening at the same time. Different staging, props, and costumes are being tried out. Performers are trying ways to move about the stage area and to project their voices so they can be heard by the audience. They are trying different tones to change their voices and experimenting with gestures. Other participants are trying different ways to manage their tasks and materials, and members of the audience are listening and thinking of comments to make during the discussion that follows. Through practices, the children begin to realize that characters and tasks can be handled in a variety of ways and they are attempting to find their best way.

After the children are more familiar with a practice, try to encourage some improvisation. Gather the children together and ask them to suggest how they can *change* or *add to* the speaking parts in the storybook. "How else could you say that? What could you do when you say that?" Discuss their ideas. Encourage them to try them. They will no doubt enjoy adding innovative words and actions and be encouraged to experiment on their own. To further support improvisation, the teacher begins to simplify the narration and depends less on the wording of the storybook. Only basic story information is provided in order to encourage the children to contribute and improvise other important details. The teacher can also offer prompting as needed to help the children respond in their own words and actions. The performance guide for *The Three Billy Goats Gruff* contains a practice walk-through for the story (p.136) which illustrates using a simplified narration and prompting to facilitate thinking and improvisation by the children.

During the practices, the teacher will also be watching for children who know the story well and can eventually assume the role of the narrator. In addition to narrating, the teacher's role in practicing is that of a supportive coach rather than a "director." Overall, practices should encourage children to think and talk about their assignments, make decisions, and try to evaluate them. Innovation is applauded both in handling a task or portraying a character. The teacher can intervene temporarily if the practice wavers, offering "outside" intervention through additional prompting comments or questions, and "inside" intervention by assuming and modeling a role or task. Overall, the teacher needs a light but steady hand during practices, while encouraging children to work through concerns together. Often teachers find it helpful to close the classroom door during practices to provide a protective environment for all.

The closing discussion is an important component of a practice as it engages the audience in a very active way. After the characters and participants reflect and briefly talk about their work, the audience questions and makes suggestions concerning the overall presentation. This can provide valuable insight, extending comprehension and identifying new dialogue and actions for future practices. The discussion also brings a comprehensive closure to the practice and eases the transition to the next activity.

Young children may need some guidance in preparing for a closing discussion. Before the first practice, talk about what the children have learned about being good speakers and listeners: "What do we see and hear if someone is a good speaker? What do we see and hear if someone is a good listener?" Then relate this to being good performers and members of the audience. Explain that the audience will have to watch the performers carefully to be able to share their comments during the discussion that follows. Model and practice how

to provide thoughtful comments by saying something you like about the drama or making a suggestion: "I really liked the Troll's grumpy voice. You could walk up the hill a little slower." Adult prompting can also help children express their ideas tactfully and respond politely to suggestions from others. "How could you say that using different words? Thank you for sharing that idea."

Together, you might compile a picture/word chart to clarify the discussion process which can be posted and used as needed during discussions. Charts usually include some of the following points which, of course, can be adapted.

Arranging practices depends largely upon the age, needs, and interests of the children, the size of the group, and the practice time possible. Again, some rotation ensures that the children have variety in their experiences. The teacher can consider alternatives, including the following, and decide what works best for a particular group.

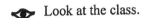

Performer:

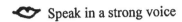 Look at the class.

Speak in a strong voice

? Tell the class when you are ready
• for questions and comments.

☞ Choose someone to speak.

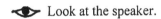

Audience:

Look at the speaker.

 Listen to what the speaker is saying.

 Think of things to tell the speaker
and how to say them kindly.

 Raise your hand when you are ready
to speak.

- Divide the children into three groups—actors, tasks, and audience—and rotate them during three different practices done at different times. Each is followed by a brief sharing time to gain insight about the different types of involvement. Remember, additional roles, tasks, and chores for the audience can always be added. A drama-minded parent might also be interested in assisting with several whole-group practices during which roles can be rotated.

- Children can perform the play, or sections of it, in small groups when the rest of the class is involved in other activities. Here again, parents can provided help. Morrow and Smith (1990) found that kindergartners who retold stories in small groups of three gained more in comprehension than those who retold stories in whole groups. For some children, a small-group approach might be very inviting.

When the improvised practices are moving smoothly, everyone can decide when they are ready to schedule the group's culminating presentation, the performance.

Although necessary prompting can be provided, a performance is a rather special *non-stop* dramatization in full costume and staging. A few extra touches can even be added, such as a parent taking individual and group photographs or serving juice and crackers afterwards for the participants. Timing the performance is a major decision, and children benefit from being involved in the decision making.

OBSERVING STORY DRAMATIZATION SKILLS

In both dramatic play and story dramatization, the teacher needs to be a skillful observer to provide appropriate guidance. Both types of pretending benefit from the use of checklists that provide specific information about the level of individual children's involvement. Such checklists offer insight concerning children's strengths and needs and are invaluable in designing and adapting teaching strategies to advance learning.

As both dramatic play and story dramatization focus on pretending, they share commonalities in observing. A number of the items in the section "Observing dramatic play skills" (Chapter 3) also apply to observing story dramatizations, so it might be helpful to review that earlier section. You will note, too, that some dramatic play skills are also included in the story dramatization skills below.

By reviewing this list, a teacher can select points of interest and create a personal checklist for observing story dramatizations. A performance scale can be established such as: Beginning/Intermediate/Advanced; or Not yet/Occasionally/Frequently; or even a numerical scale from low (1) to high (5). The design of dramatic play and story dramatization checklists depend on what the teacher needs to know to plan effectively for a particular group. Additional skills can be added to observe specific participants such as the student narrator, prop and costume manager, and even members of the audience.

Story dramatization skills

- How convincingly does she portray the role of the character being performed?

- Is he able to remain in character for the duration of the dramatization?

- Does she use effective facial and body gestures and voices for the characters being performed?

- Can he improvise in portraying the role of the character?

- Does she always prefer the same roles?

- Does he use props effectively?

- Does she exchange ideas with others about the play?

- Does he maintain appropriate eye contact with other players?

- Can her speech be heard and understood?

- Does he use varied tones of voice when interacting with other players?

- Does she sometimes lead/sometimes follow others?

- Is he flexible when interacting with other players?

DECIDING ABOUT A PERFORMANCE FOR OTHERS

The decision whether to present a performance for an invited audience requires some thought, with basic considerations being the age and maturity of the group. Younger children, such as three-year-olds, can be cautious and move at their own pace. They often begin pretending by simply chorusing parts of a nursery rhyme with their teacher and perhaps adding a few body movements. Then they may move to acting out parts of a familiar story as the teacher reads the story. As the year progresses, the children could be ready to learn the beginning story, *The Three Billy Goats Gruff* (Chapter 6) and enjoy doing several casual practices with simple props. As this story is quite brief and designed for introducing story dramatization, a special performance or a performance for others might not be planned. Often, practices are enough for young children and as far as they want to venture. The final practice *becomes their performance*. But what about more adventurous threes, fours, fives, and older children? Momentum is more obvious, and the idea of a performance for guests becomes exciting as enthusiasm mounts for sharing their experience with others.

There are still other things to consider in deciding about a performance with guests. The needs and interests of the children are of primary importance, but such basics as preparation, space, time, and parent assistance are influential. It is essential in deciding, however, *not* to equate a performance by young children with a theatrical event by older children. A performance by young children does not involve overwhelming details or unending practices, but rather is minimal and child-centered both in preparation and delivery. Such a performance has few basic needs and is manageable because the dramatic quality is not the main focus of the presentation. Rather, that focus is what the children are learning by being involved, and it is important that guests understand this. If a performance for others is decided upon, the children simply practice until it is agreed that the story is ready to perform for friends. Then relax and remember that the audience will be child-friendly. Whether it is the custodian, the office staff, or parents and grandparents, the audience will include people who enjoy the children. Regardless of what happens on the stage, the audience will think the performers are absolutely marvelous and applaud loudly.

Now, how can a performance for guests be arranged? As always there are choices:

- As the play *The Three Billy Goats Gruff* is fairly brief, it is possible to plan two or more performances for different audiences that might include parents, the school office staff, or another classroom. Add a bit of flare by including more participants as ticket collectors or ushers.

- As the play is brief, you can rotate groups of performers, participants, and audiences and take the show on the road to several other classrooms in the building. The room audience can join the audience of the other classroom and be ready to model and share comments at the end.

- Arrange to have some performances videotaped by a parent so that a CD can be sent home and shared with family members or even out-of-town grandparents. Be sure to include views of *all* of the participants performing their tasks, *including the audience.*

Part 3

THE PERFORMANCE

Curtain Going Up!

By having several practices and performances over a few weeks, children are able to be involved in a variety of assignments. Still, there is always the question of who does what for a final performance that seems "special". Sometimes it is not a concern because children rather naturally slip into a position which is satisfying to them. Where there is concern about a popular role or task, you can always resort to a lottery draw; although there might be some disappointment, most young children recognize that this process is a fair one.

Chapter 6

PERFORMANCE GUIDE FOR DRAMATIZING
THE THREE BILLY GOATS GRUFF

Now, having studied the section on preparing a story dramatization in Chapter 5, it's time to plan and dramatize *The Three Billy Goats Gruff*. The curtain will soon be "going up"—a pretend one, of course.

This section contains a comprehensive guide to practicing and performing a first story, *The Three Billy Goats Gruff*, and includes an illustrated storybook to use as a basis for storytelling, reading, and picture-reading, along with suggestions for hands-on activities. A walk-through practice illustrates the use of teacher prompting to help children begin improvising, using their own words and actions. Although the guide is designed to assist teachers in initial planning, the suggestions can also be adopted or adapted in future dramatizations.

Take time to become familiar with the picture storybook *The Three Billy Goats Gruff* and just enjoy it. It is not only beautiful but eye-catching and quite different. The striking illustrations are silhouettes done in color which convey the story in a straightforward manner and complement the text. The large-size, double-page illustrations are easy for young children to view and handle. The text can help teachers in planning to *tell* the story and the storybook can then be *read* and *picture-read* with the children. Another benefit of the storybook is that additional copies can be downloaded and printed at school for classroom and home use (see www.jkp.com).

The storybook text

Once upon a time, there were three billy goats who were brothers and their last name was Gruff. There was Billy Goat One who was the smallest goat, there was Billy Goat Two who was the middle-size goat, and there was Billy Goat Three who was the largest goat.

The Three Billy Goats Gruff lived on the rocky side of a hill so they wanted to go across a bridge and eat the delicious grass on the other side, but a terrible troll lived under the bridge and he was very mean.

One day, Billy Goat One walked on the bridge and the bridge made a funny sound, trip trap, trip trap! The Troll heard the noise and roared: "Who is walking on my bridge? I am going to eat you up." "Please don't eat me up," said the smallest billy goat. "Wait for Billy Goat Two. He will taste much better." So the Troll let Billy Goat One walk across the bridge and eat the grass on the other side.

Then Billy Goat Two walked on the bridge and the bridge made a funny sound, trip trap, trip trap! The Troll heard the noise and roared: "Who is walking on my bridge? I am going to eat you up." "Please don't eat me up," said the middle-sized billy goat. "Wait for Billy Goat Three. He will taste much better." So the Troll let Billy Goat Two walk across the bridge and eat the grass on the other side.

Then Billy Goat Three walked on the bridge and the bridge made a funny sound, trip trap, trip trap! The Troll heard the noise and roared: "Who is walking on my bridge? I am going to eat you up."

But Billy Goat Three was the largest and strongest billy goat and he walked down to the Troll and, with his big horns, gave the Troll a giant bump. The Troll flew into the air and was gone forever.

Then the Three Billy Goats Gruff ate the delicious grass on the other side of the hill.

The End

Literacy links

As you become familiar with the text and plan the oral reading and picture reading, take note of opportunities for literacy learning involved in the story. Re-examine "The literacy connection" in Chapter 1 and include learning opportunities when teachable moments arise. They can often be slipped in or reinforced as the children prepare for the dramatization. The following is a sampling of such literacy-related opportunities.

1. New vocabulary:

silhouette	actor	scenery	props
practice	performance	billy goat	smallest
horn	hooves	beard	middle-size
troll	bump	across	largest-size
rocky	delicious	roar	grass

2. Initial consonants:

   /b/ as in billy

   /g/ as in goat

   /m/ as in mean

As children look at copies of the storybook, they can move page by page and have a letter hunt to find words that begin with initial consonants. These can be recorded and counted, and the findings compared.

3. Initial consonant blends:

   /tr/ as in troll, trip, trap

   /gr/ as in gruff, grass

   /br/ as in bridge

Children can name words *not* in the storybook that also begin with these initial consonant blends.

4. Word families:

   /ump/ as in bump

   /ip/ as in trip

   /ap/ as in trap

   /ing/ as in going

   /est/ as in strongest

Children can make new words by using different

beginning sounds, such as:

> ump: bump, dump, hump, jump, lump, pump
>
> ip: dip, hip, lip, rip, sip, tip
>
> ap: cap, gap, lap, map, nap, rap, sap, tap
>
> ing: king, ping, ring, sing, wing
>
> est: best, jest, nest, pest, rest, test, vest, west.

5. Repetitive sentences:

> Trip trap, trip trap!
>
> Who is walking on my bridge?
>
> I am going to eat you up!

Write a repetitive story sentence on two separate strips of tagboard and cut one strip into word sections. Children can arrange the cut sections into a sentence, using the uncut strip as a guide, if needed. Pieces can be stored in a ziplock bag.

LEARNING THIS STORY
Telling

Story dramatization begins with knowing the story, and telling, reading, and picture-reading *The Three Billy Goats Gruff* can help accomplish this. Being experienced with reading stories, teachers may be inclined to start by reading the story. This can be done, of course, but it is highly preferable to *tell* the story first so that children can visualize it in their imagination. By mentally constructing their own version of the story, it becomes more embedded and personally meaningful.

After becoming familiar with the storybook, think about the different details you can dramatize in telling the story. Carefully review the general planning suggestions concerning storytelling (Chapter 5) and adapt them in telling this story to your group. You might begin by introducing the word "troll," clarifying it and explaining that this troll was mean and did not know how to share. You might ask related questions such as "What things do we share at school?" or "What things are hard to share?"

Slip into telling the story, using your own words and gestures to paint a vivid picture of the setting, characters, and events. You could emphasize the barren, rocky side of the hill and contrast it with the tasty green grass on the other hill. The differences in size, voice, and gestures of the three goats could be contrasted. You might describe their horns, their tails, their hooves, or illustrate with blocks the noise the bridge makes as they cross. Convey the repetitive flow of words and story events along with the surprising ending in an engaging manner that captures and holds the children's attention. It is simply a good story, and telling it enables you to embellish it. Follow the story with a few questions that stimulate thinking, the exchange of ideas, and strengthen comprehension. For example:

- What do you think was the problem?
- How did Billy Goat Three solve the problem?
- Do you think that was a good idea? Why?
- Can anyone think of another way?
- What can we do to share things in our class?

Use helpful ideas such as "Let's use it together," "take turns," "wait patiently for your turn," or "ask for help."

Older children might talk about "tattling" as opposed to helpful telling.

Reading and picture-reading

Figure 6.1: Picture-reading the storybook

Reconsider the general planning suggestions about reading and picture-reading in Chapter 5, and how you can apply them to this story. You might begin by having the children look at the cover and try to guess the name of the book. They might be surprised that the story you told them earlier is also written in a book. You could explain that stories can be told in different ways and that they can tell the story by pretending and acting out what happens.

Look at the illustrations: "How are these pictures different from other pictures in our library books?" A new vocabulary word, "silhouette," could be introduced. When ready, dramatically read the story. As the children are already familiar with it, they can add comments or notice some similarities and differences during the reading.

Invite the children to tell the story themselves. "Now, it's your turn to tell this story by 'reading' the pictures in the book. You can tell us in your own words what a picture tells you about the story. Let's look at the cover. What do you think this book is about?" Encourage the children to continue telling the story page by page in their way while you listen or, if needed, add a bit of support. "What happens next? Yes, you're reading the pictures." If more prompting is needed, try some of the following questions or your own to keep the retelling moving.

- Storybook pp.1–2, tell us about the animals in the picture. How do you think they are different?

- Storybook pp.3–4, look at all the rocks on this side. How is the land on the other side of the bridge different?

- Storybook pp.5–6, tell us about the Troll. How does he look?

- Storybook pp.7–8, tell us about the goat walking on the bridge. What kind of noise could the bridge make? What do you think the Troll and Billy Goat One are saying to each other?

- Storybook pp.9–10, tell us what is happening now. Where is Billy Goat One? Why? Tell us what you think the Troll and Billy Goat Two are talking about.

- Storybook pp.10–11, what does Billy Goat Three want to do? What do you think the Troll is telling the largest goat? What do you think is going to happen? What happened?

- Storybook pp.12–13, now what are the three goats doing? How do you think the goats feel? Where do you think the Troll could have gone?

The Three Billy Goats Gruff

Retold by Carol Woodard

Illustrations by Suzanne Mair

Once upon a time, there were three billy goats who were brothers and their last name was Gruf

1   There was Billy Goat One who was the smallest goat, there was Billy Goat Two who was the

middle-size goat, and there was Billy Goat Three who was the largest goat.

The Three Billy Goats Gruff lived on the rocky side of a hill so they wanted to go across a bridge and eat the delicious grass on the other side,

3

but a terrible troll lived under the bridge and he was very mean.

4

One day, Billy Goat One walked on the bridge and the bridge made a funny sound, trip trap, trip trap! The Troll heard the noise and roared: "Who is walking on my bridge? I am going to eat you up."

"Please don't eat me up," said the smallest billy goat. "Wait for Billy Goat Two. He will taste much better."

So the Troll let Billy Goat One walk across the bridge and eat the grass on the other side.

Then Billy Goat Two walked on the bridge and the bridge made a funny sound, trip trap, trip trap! The Troll heard the noise and roared: "Who is walking on my bridge? I am going to eat you up."

"Please don't eat me up," said the middle-sized billy goat.

"Wait for Billy Goat Three. He will taste much better."

So the Troll let Billy Goat Two walk across the bridge and eat the grass on the other side.

8

Then Billy Goat Three walked on the bridge and the bridge made a funny sound, trip trap, trip trap!

9

The Troll heard the noise and roared:

"Who is walking on my bridge?

I am going to eat you up."

10

But Billy Goat Three was the largest and strongest billy goat and he walked down to the Troll and, with his big horns, gave the Troll a giant bump.

The Troll flew into the air and was gone forever.

13   Then the Three Billy Goats Gruff ate the delicious grass

on the other side of the hill. The End

PICTURE READING PROMPTING SUGGESTIONS (CHOOSE ACCORDING TO DEVELOPMENTAL LEVEL

Cover: What do you think this story is about?
How many animals do you see?

pp.1–2 Tell us about the animals in the picture.
How are they different?

pp.3–4 How does the land on this side (p.3) look?
How is it different to this side (p.4)?
How does the troll look?

pp.5–6 Tell us about the goat walking on the bridge.
What kind of noise does the bridge make?
What do you think the troll and Billy goat One are saying to each other?
What happens?

pp.7–8 What is Billy Goat One doing now?
Where is Billy Goat Two?
What do you think the troll and Billy Goat Two are talking about?
What happens?

pp.9–10 What are Billy Goats One and Two doing now?
Who is walking on the bridge?
What do you think the troll is telling BIlly Goat Three?
Why do you think the troll doesn't want the goats to go across the bridge?
What do you think is going to happen?

pp.11–12 What does happen?

pp.13–14 Now what are all the three goats doing?
How do you think they feel?
Where do you think the troll could have gone (or might have learned)?

Remember to compliment the children's picture-reading efforts and to provide copies of the storybook for classroom use so they can enjoy picture reading to each other. Other copies can be sent home with a simple note about the value of picture reading.

OPTIONAL FLANNELBOARD RETELLING

For an additional retelling, a flannelboard is an appealing method because the storyteller simply places pictures from the story on a flannelboard (See "How to make a folding flannelboard," Chapter 5) as the story is being told. Children are usually intrigued and eager to try it, and it is fairly easy for them to manage after observing the teacher using it.

When the teacher tells a flannelboard story to a whole group, some basic organization is useful in holding the children's attention. Teachers often sequence the pictures in a pile beforehand, with the first one to be used on top and the last used on the bottom, and practice with the pictures to determine the best placement of the pictures on the board. When ready, retell the story and move the pictures on/off the board to correspond with the storyline. Pictures no longer being used can be placed under or behind the board.

When the story is retold again, the children can become involved by placing pictures on the board and narrating parts or the whole story. Following the retellings, the materials are placed in an area where the children can take turns using the flannelboard to tell the story to each other. Two children can use it together by one telling the story while the other arranges the figures, and then reversing roles. Their approach with the materials will likely be much less organized and more casual. The children may just spread the pictures around the board and search for what is needed to tell the tale. Partners often help in the searching and join in the telling. Be sure to have a copy of the storybook nearby for reference. In the beginning, the children will probably need time to just manipulate the materials, and perhaps some individual guidance to get started.

Flannelboard pictures

The pictures (p.131) are provided for the flannelboard retelling of *The Three Billy Goats Gruff*, followed by easy directions for mounting them. These directions can also be used to make flannelboard pictures for other stories by simply copying pictures of the main characters and objects from the storybook and mounting them.

Mounting the flannelboard pictures

1. If possible, laminate the pictures as this will help preserve them.

2. Spray-glue the picture page to lightweight tag board or the cardboard backing from a large writing pad and cut the outlined pictures apart.

3. Glue a medium-sized strip of coarse sandpaper to the back of each picture so it will adhere to the flannel on the board. A strip of felt material can be used instead of sandpaper.

ROLES AND TASKS

Look over the general planning suggestions in "Ways to participate" (Chapter 5), and consider with the children the different ways they can be involved in the dramatization. "Can you think of another animal that could be on the stage? Could the Troll have a grouchy dog? What could we name him?"

Suggestions

Acting roles for which the children volunteer:

- narrator
- the Troll
- Billy Goat One
- Billy Goat Two
- Billy Goat Three
- other: pretend trees, clumps of grass, rocks, the sun, flowers, a dog, bird, or rabbit.

Participant roles for which the children volunteer:

- sound effects staff
- chorus for repetitive phrases
- prop/costume staff
- audience
- photographer
- sign holder ("clap" or "applause")
- prompter.

Flannelboard figures for *The Three Billy Goats Gruff*

SIMPLE STAGING

Talk over how to make the stage look like the place in the story: "What do we need? How can we make it? Where could we get it?"

Suggestions

- Obtain several fairly large cardboard boxes on which the children can paint rocks, green grass, birds, forest animals, etc., to make scenery for around the bridge. Small paper plates could be painted as flowers and pasted on the boxes. Dandelions and other familiar flowers are often available to examine and discuss, adding a touch of science. The children can then paint their own flower versions on the boxes or paper plates.

- Paint an old sheet with hills, trees, rocks, and grass, and hang it across a clothesline tied to two sturdy chairs.

- Hollow blocks and a walking board can be used to make a bridge. If these are not available, two pieces of masking or electrical tape can be placed parallel to each other on the floor to create a pretend bridge.

- Place adult chairs on each side of the bridge and cover with old sheets to represent the hills. Rocks might be painted on one and grass on the other.

- For a very basic hill, tape sheets of construction paper on the wall and add fringed sections of colored paper for the grass (Figure 6.2).

Figure 6.2: Staging a hill with grass

- Tape a piece of sturdy cardboard on the floor and paint to represent water below the bridge, adding rocks, fish, or a turtle. A firm, non-skid bath mat could also be used to represent the water.

- Create a scary house for the Troll by painting a cardboard box with some spooky creative artwork.

- Remember the possibility of adding some non-speaking roles such as children curled up to represent large rocks, or holding homemade flowers, or moving strips of paper representing grass. You could even adapt the storyline to include a child pretending to be a breeze blowing through.

CASUAL PROPS AND COSTUMES

Review the general planning suggestions concerning props and costumes in Chapter 5 to involve the children further. Their ideas can be innovative and endless! "What do you think a troll would wear? How about a pair of dark glasses and some rain boots good for stamping?" Halloween leftovers can provide more possibilities.

"How can the goats look furry?" A chenille bath mat over the shoulders might do the trick.

Suggestions

- For sound effects, chorus members can use blocks or rhythm sticks, or stamp their feet to make the "trip trap" sounds.

- Make a goat headband (Figure 6.3). Use sturdy construction paper strips (about 2 inches/5 cm wide and 24 inches/60 cm long) for the headbands. Children sometimes like to write the numeral 1, 2, or 3, in the middle of the headband to identify their favorite goat. They can draw two horns free-hand on construction paper or trace around a triangular shape about $3 \times 3 \times 2$ inches ($7.5 \times 7.5 \times 5$ cm) made from the cardboard backing from a large writing pad. They then cut the two horns from the construction paper and staple them to the sides of the headband. When the horns are attached, the headband ends are securely taped according to head size.

Figure 6.3: Boys making goat head bands

- Make a fierce face mask. Begin by talking about angry faces using a good-size mirror for viewing. The children can decorate a large paper plate with their version of a mean face and attach it to a sturdy paint stirrer with masking tape for holding. Paint stirrers are often available without charge at paint stores. This type of mask can be held in front of the face, or worn over the face by attaching a narrow elastic band (Figure 6.4).

Figure 6.4: Boy wearing a face mask

- Add a flowing towel cape for the Troll and a floppy hat.

- Create a goat beard by taping rubber bands (to place around the child's ears) on two adjoining corners of a white wash cloth.

- Add some bells if available as goats often wear bells. ("Why?")

- Make a numeral sign (1, 2, 3) for the performing goats to wear taped to their shirt fronts to identify them.

- Create grass to wave by pasting strips of paper to a paint stirrer or paper towel holder.

PRACTICING, PROMPTING, AND IMPROVISING

First, look through the general planning suggestions concerning practicing in Chapter 5. Initially, the teacher narrates using the familiar storybook text and the children generally follow the storybook dialogue to portray the characters. During subsequent practices,

however, both the teacher and children move away from the words of the storybook text and rely more on improvisation. To do this, the teacher begins to simplify the narration by providing only basic information and using prompting comments to help the children think of their own words and actions to tell the story. The children have already previously talked about how dialogue can be changed or extended to enliven a dramatization so they should be ready to venture out on their own. If additional help is needed, the teacher can temporarily assume a character role and model some acting.

The following practice walk-through for *The Three Billy Goats Gruff* uses a simplified narration and prompting comments to illustrate this approach. These suggestions, however, are merely possibilities. Narrating and prompting depends on the needs, interests, and developmental levels of the children, and each teacher will develop an individual plan. Peers also offer ideas during practices, but it is the child in character who needs to decide what to say and do. There are, however, degrees of improvisation. Younger children who like familiar things may prefer to stay close to the storyline text in their practices. In contrast, older children tend to flow with the simplified narration and extend and adjust their dialogue and actions to the words of others. They enjoy the challenge of improvising the story and may invent unique versions that change the story considerably. Teacher prompting can also spark new ideas. For example, the Troll and the goats might negotiate a compromise about sharing the grasslands. Innovative versions reflect thinking and merit recognition. For a special performance, the children can vote on which version to present.

Teacher intervention is generally minimal and each rehearsal will be a little different according to the unique interpretations of the individual participants.

A PRACTICE WALK-THROUGH
Narration
Once upon a time there were three billy goats who were brothers and their last name was Gruff.

Prompting suggestions (if needed)

- (To goats) you could begin by introducing yourself.

- What else could you tell about yourself? (e.g. different sizes, perhaps wearing different colored hats or bells)

Figure 6.5: Children with masks dramatizing The Three Billy Goats Gruff

Narration

The Three Billy Goats Gruff lived on the rocky side of a hill so they wanted to go across a bridge to eat the delicious grass on the other side, but a mean and nasty troll lived under the bridge.

Prompting suggestions (if needed)

- Troll, you need to tell us who you are.

- What else could you tell about yourself? (e.g. the troll is mean and crabby, lives under the bridge, doesn't like to share)

- How would your face look if you were mean and crabby?

- Grasses, you could wave a little so we notice you.

Narration

One day Billy Goat One walked on the bridge and the bridge made a funny sound, trip trap, trip, trap.

Prompting suggestions (if needed)

- Where do you walk, Billy Goat One?

- Chorus, what kind of sound do you make when Billy Goat One walks on the bridge?

Narration

The Troll heard the noise and roared.

Prompting suggestions (if needed)

- Troll, what could you say to scare Billy Goat One?

- How could you sound really mean?

- What does Billy Goat One tell the Troll about his bigger brother?

Narration

So the Troll let Billy Goat One walk across the bridge and eat the grass on the other side. Then Billy Goat Two walked on the bridge and the bridge made a funny sound, trip, trap, trip trap.

Prompting suggestions (if needed)

- Chorus, what sound do you make again?

- Billy Goat One, what are you busy doing now?

- Where are you going now, Billy Goat Two?

- What could the Troll and Billy Goat Two say to each other?

Narration

So the Troll let Billy Goat Two walk across the bridge and eat the grass on the other side. Then Billy Goat Three walked on the bridge and the bridge made a funny sound. (Chorus provides sound effects.)

Prompting suggestions (if needed)

- Billy Goat Two, where have you gone and what are you eating?

- What do you do, Billy Goat Three?

- Now the Troll and Billy Goat Three have an angry talk. What could you say to each other?

Narration

But Billy Goat Three was the largest and strongest billy goat and with his big horns gave the Troll a giant bump. The Troll flew into the air and was gone forever.

Prompting suggestions (if needed)

- Billy Goat Three, what could you say and do to show us that you are really big and strong?

- What could the Troll tell Billy Goat Three?

- Billy Goat Three, what could you tell the Troll?

- How can you show there is a really big bump? (For example, a walk-on sign reading "Bump!" or a drum roll, or a cymbal tap, a chorus chant: BUMP!)

- Troll, how could you move to show you're flying through the air?

Narration

Then the three Billy Goats Gruff ate all the delicious grass on the other side of the hill.

Prompting suggestions (if needed)

- How could the goats show they were very happy to eat the grass together? (For example, sing new words to a familiar song and circle about holding hands.)

Narration

The End

Curtain call: Bows and applause for everyone following the practice walk-through (Figure 6.6).

The closing discussion following a practice provides an opportunity for both characters and participants to offer comments guided by the performer/audience chart suggestions on p.117. The cast might tell what they liked best about their work, or what they could do differently, or even what they learned. In turn, the audience can ask questions and offer suggestions. In a final performance for invited guests, the discussion might simply consist of well-deserved accolades from the audience for the hard-working presenters.

Figure 6.6: Children taking a bow after the practice walk-through

When they have mastered this version of the storybook, children sometimes like to hear or even dramatize a different picture storybook version. Other versions to consider include:

Carpenter, S. (1998) *The Three Billy Goats Gruff*. New York, NY: HarperCollins. This version is for the very young.

Gladone, P. (1973) *The Three Billy Goats*. New York, NY: Clarion Books.

Granowsky, A. (1995) *The Three Billy Goats Gruff / Just a Friendly Old Troll (Another Point of View)*. New York, NY: Steck-Vaughn.

STORY-RELATED ACTIVITIES

The following optional activities can be simplified or extended as needed for individual, partner, and small- or whole-group use.

Picture/word cards for writing

Photocopy another set of the flannelboard figures on p.131 and clearly print the name of the object below each picture: goat 1, goat 2, goat 3, bridge, grass, and troll. Laminate if possible. Cut the figures apart as outlined and spray-glue each to 5 × 8 inch (12.5 × 20 cm) cards. Paper-punch each card and tie on a shoelace (Figure 6.7). Using the word cards as a resource, children can draw and write about the dramatization in their own way.

Figure 6.7: Picture/word cards

Story box

This story can easily be retold by using a story box (see Chapter 5). Parents can help gather plastic goats and a troll, or the children might like to make casual figures from clay. These can be placed in the block area or used on a table to manipulate and explore, with the children retelling the story in their own way. If goats are not available, substitute three dinosaurs or polar bears or whatever you have for figures and adapt the story. The children will likely find the substitutions amusing.

Troll cups

The children can use magic markers to decorate Styrofoam cups with mean troll faces. Then they can fill the cup with potting soil and plant grass seed. Names should be written on the cups with a permanent marker. The children can water the plants using a squirt bottle, watch their troll grow green hair, and even give it a haircut (Figure 6.8). Add more science by observing extra grass cups which are grown with/without water and with/without light. Parents often enjoy assisting gardening activities.

Figure 6.8: Troll cups with grass growing

Adapt a song

Using the melody of a familiar song such as "The bear went over the mountain," change the words to fit this story. For example: "Trip trap over the bridge, trip trap over the bridge, trip trap over the bridge, I'm going to eat you up."

Goat facts

Show the children the large picture of a goat (Figure 6.9), and talk about some of the following interesting facts concerning them:

- Goats have hooves with two parts instead of feet.

- They have tails that often turn up.

- Most goats have beards.

- Some goats have horns that are twisted and grow backwards.

- A boy goat is called a "billy goat" and a girl goat is called a "nanny goat".

- Nanny goats give milk like a cow gives milk. Their milk can be made into goat cheese.

- If there are a lot of goats, they are called a "herd" of goats.

- Some goats wear bells so the person taking care of them can find them if they get lost.

After the discussion, you or a parent might like to serve a snack of crackers with a small taste of goat cheese on top. Some facts might also be written on a picture/word chart for older children to read.

Paper roll story

Tape a roll of white shelf paper along one area of classroom wall and divide the paper into sections, briefly labeling each as to what happens sequentially in the story. The children draw their own version of the pictures for each story section and then picture-read their story by moving along from section to section and perhaps adding some dramatization.

Take home flannelboard

Parent volunteers can make a small-size flannelboard inside a box to send home on a rotating basis so that each child can retell the story at home (Figure 6.10). Obtain a sturdy box with a lid approximately 10×15 inches (25×38 cm). Using spray adhesive, line the inside bottom of the box using black, white, or light blue flannel cloth. To make the story figures, simply follow the directions on p.130 for mounting the flannelboard pictures for this

Figure 6.9: A goat

story. Place the figures inside the box and glue a copy of the story on the inside of the box lid. Place the box in an easy-to-carry shopping bag and write on the outside: "Please listen to me tell this story."

Figure 6.10: Take-home flannelboard box

HOME-BASED LITERACY ACTIVITIES

Choose from the following age-appropriate activities which can be included when communicating with parents to illustrate ways they can become active home teachers.

LISTENING ACTIVITIES

- Go to different places with your child such as the park, the playground, or the lake. Listen and identify different kinds of sounds: the cry of a baby, the meow of a kitten, the roar of a motorcycle, and the wail of a fire siren. Recognizing different sounds helps children hear sounds in words.

- When reading a story to your child, stop and ask some questions to encourage careful listening. "Why didn't the bunny want to live in the bird's nest?"

- Give three or four simple directions and have your child carry them out. "Go into the back hall, hang up your coat, and put your backpack on the kitchen table."

- Give me a rhyme! Give the child a word or sentence and ask him to give you a word or sentence that rhymes.

- Have your child listen carefully to suggestions that can be used to solve a problem. "Ask Carsen to pass the scissors to you. You can tell Cooper that you were using the truck."

- What is it? "I am thinking of a word that begins with the first sound in 'run' and it's the name of an animal that hops." Answer: rabbit.

- Listen with your child to a story on tape and, when finished, ask the child to tell what happened first, next, last.

- What sound do you hear? During spare seconds, give the child a word and ask what sound is heard at the start or end of the word. Begin with easy-to-identify sounds like "m" as in Mother or "d" as in Dad. Other easier sounds to identify are: f, j, k, l, n, r, s, t, v.

- Play "Pack your Suitcase." Begin by saying, "I am going on a trip and in my suitcase I'm putting my toothbrush." The child then repeats the sentence and adds one more item. Take turns repeating all the items in the suitcase, including the new one. When you can list five or six items, you are a winner and, of course, you can have two winners.

- Play games that involve listening and following specific directions, similar to "Simon says": "Jump twice, run around the tree, and sit on the bottom step."

TALKING ACTIVITIES

- Use questions that start with "how," "what," "when," "where," "why," and "which," because they encourage children to think and talk more when responding.

- Extend speech. Listen to what your child is saying and add a related idea to expand the conversation. "Yes, you're painting the troll's head" can be extended by adding "and orange is really an unusual color for his hair."

- Encourage drama by providing miniatures of real objects such as people, farm and zoo animals, furniture, and cars, which can be used on a table top for pretending with a friend. Also, a box with hats, goggles, gloves, a briefcase, a lunchbox, purses, shoes, etc. can foster pretending and talking. If you briefly join the play, speak to the child in the role the child has assumed.

- Watch TV together and discuss what was viewed. Compare two characters, discuss cause and effect, or talk about "what would happen if…"

- Use language to solve problems. Identify the problem, then talk about ways of solving it and the possible consequences. Choose a solution and try it out. Then talk some more.

- Be alert to words that are unfamiliar to the child. Talk about what they mean, provide synonyms, and use new words often so they become part of the child's vocabulary. Try acting out a new word to make the meaning more visual.

- Remediate a child's error using a sound or word by simply correcting and repeating it to the child without comment. "Yes, the car is yellow" (for "lellow"). Often it helps a child to pronounce a troublesome word by having it broken into syllables—for example, "rec-i-pe."

- When you and your child go shopping, stop and carefully look at the things in a window display. Holiday toy displays are especially interesting. Walk away and ask your child to tell you everything that was seen. It's also fun to go back and look again.

- Include your child in mealtime conversations. "Tell me about your favorite thing that happened at school today. Tell me what you like best about the new kitten."

- Include the child in tasks that can be enjoyed, such as washing the car with Dad, and introduce several new vocabulary words while doing the tasks.

WRITING ACTIVITIES
Suggestion

- Provide parents with a copy of handwriting-style printing of both upper- and lower-case letters of the alphabet to use with children.

- Arrange a writing spot for the child. Place in a shoebox basic materials such as lined and unlined paper, pencils, magic markers, crayons, blunt-tip scissors, and paste.

- Print the child's name with a wide magic marker in letters about 2.5 inches (6 cm) across the center of the cardboard backing from a large writing pad. Slip the pad back into a transparent file folder. Using a wipe off crayon, the child can practice writing his name over or below the model and erase it with a dry washcloth.

- Print the child's name in the upper left corner of drawings and suggest the child could print it there too. Ask the child if she would like you to write the name of an item in the drawing, such as "tree."

- Take pictures of a few toys the child has selected as "favorites." Paste them in a scrapbook and print the name of each item below. The child can "read" the book to a grandparent or friend.

- Together, write a thank-you note for a gift the child received. The word "thanks" and a drawing of the item can say it all.

- Have the child draw, dictate, or write a simple note to mail to a friend or relative.

- Involve the child in making a simple grocery list by drawing, dictating, or printing several favorite items for the list. They can also cut pictures of advertised items from the newspaper and search for them in the store.

- Cut a strip of tagboard about 2 × 8 inches (5 × 20 cm) and create a bookmark. The child can decorate and "write" his name on the bookmark. Provide a 3 × 5 inch (7.5 × 12.5 cm) name card for reference if needed.

- Display your child's "writing" and have it "read" to you by the child.

- Outdoors, place a layer of wet sand on a baking sheet with a rim and let your child write letters and words in it. Print some favorite words on 3 × 5 inch (7.5 × 12.5 cm) cards to use as a model. Finger paint can also be used for writing on a white oilcloth table cover.

READING ACTIVITIES

- Draw attention to familiar signs in the environment such as "Stop," "Go," "Entrance," "Exit." Point out letters and logos on familiar labels, boxes, and magazine advertisements.

- Print a sign with your child's picture and name for her bedroom door. Label several areas in the bedroom that are important to the child such as books, trucks, and desk. For younger children, have a drawing or photograph before the identifying word.

- For emergent readers, slip a simple note using familiar words into your child's lunchbox.

- Cut the front panel from an empty box of your child's favorite cereal. Use it to "read" and locate the cereal at the grocery store. Limit the searching by indicating the area in which the cereal boxes are found.

- Obtain a different version of a favorite storybook at the library and talk about the similarities and differences.

- Encourage your child to draw, dictate, or write about a special experience he has had and then "read" the work to you.

- Picture-read books without words from the library.

- Make a simple (few ingredients) recipe card with a line-drawn picture before each ingredient. Read and make the recipe together.

- Fold 5 × 8 inch (12.5 × 20 cm) cards lengthwise and print the name of each family member on a card. Have your child "read" the name of the person and place it where the person sits at dinner. For younger children, place a small photo before the name on the card.

- List the child's weekly jobs. Use picture reading if needed, such as having a simple drawing of a waste basket with the words "empty the basket."

When parents become involved in these activities early in the school year, they begin to see how the various strands of literacy weave together when learning to read.

CHILD-SIZE PUPPET OUTLINES

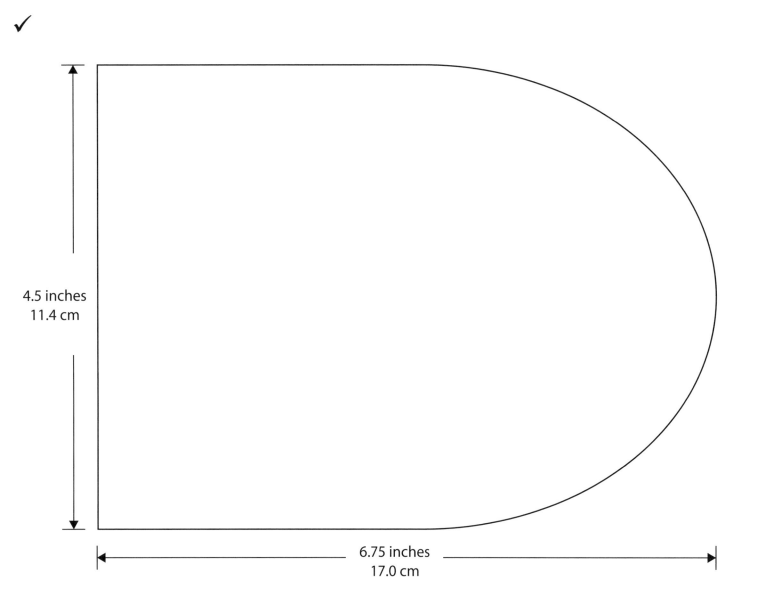

4.5 inches
11.4 cm

6.75 inches
17.0 cm

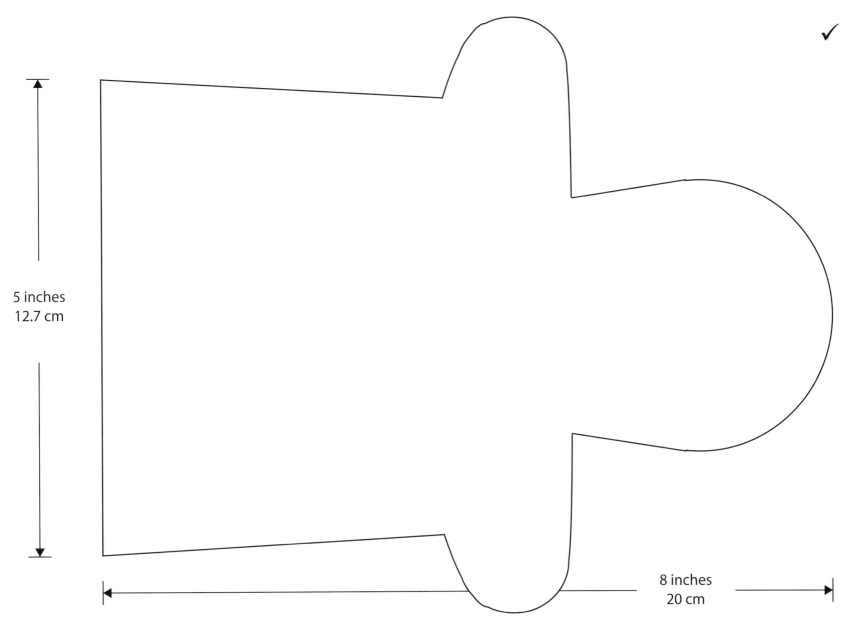

5 inches
12.7 cm

8 inches
20 cm

BIBLIOGRAPHY

Avgitidou, S. (2001) "Peer culture and friendship relationships as contexts for the development of young children's pre-social behavior." *International Journal of Early Years Education 9*, 2, 145–52.

Barclay, K. (2010) "Using song picture books to support early literacy development." *Childhood Education 86*, 3, 138–45.

Beals, D., DeTemple, J., and Dickinson, D. (1994) "Talking and Listening That Support Early Literacy Development of Children From Low-Income Families." In D. Dickinson (ed.) *Bridges to Literacy.* Cambridge: Blackwell Publishers.

Berk, L. (1994) "Vygotsky's theory: The importance of make-believe play." *Young Children*, November, 30–39.

Bodrova, E. and Leong, D. (2003) "Building language and literacy through play." *Scholastic Early Childhood Today 28*, 2, 34–7.

Bordan, S. (1970) *Plays as Teaching Tools in the Elementary School.* New York, NY: Parker.

Burns, S., Griffin, P., and Snow, C.E. (1999) *Starting Out Right: A Guide to Promoting Children's Reading Success.* Washington, DC: National Academy Press.

Christie, J. (1990) "Dramatic play: A context for meaningful engagements." *The Reading Teacher*, April, 542–5.

Cooper, P. (2009) *The Classrooms All Young Children Need: Lessons in Teaching from Vivian Paley.* Chicago, IL: University of Chicago Press.

Creech, N. and Bhavnagri, N. (2002) "Teaching elements of story through drama to first graders." *Childhood Education 78*, 4, 219–23.

Dickinson, D. (2001) "Large-Group and Free-Play Times: Conversational Settings Supporting Language and Literacy Development." In D. Dickinson and P. Tabors (eds) *Beginning Literacy with Language.* Baltimore, MD: Brookes.

Dickinson, D. and Sprague, E. (2002) "The Nature and Impact of Early Childhood Care Environments on the Language and Early Literacy Development of Children from Low-Income Families." In S. Neuman and D. Dickinson (eds) *Handbook of Early Literacy Research.* New York, NY: Guilford Press.

Forman, E.A. (1987) "Learning through peer interaction: A Vygotskian perspective." *Genetic Epistemologist*, 15, 6–15.

Fraser, K. (1968) *Stilts, Somersaults, and Headstands.* New York: Atheneum Press.

Furman, L. (2000) "In support of drama in early childhood education, again." *Early Childhood Education Journal 27*, 3, 173–8.

Gardner, H. (1983) *Frames of Mind: The Theory of Multiple Intelligences.* New York, NY: Basic/HarperCollins.

Hakkarainen, P. (2002) *Developmental Pre-School Education and Learning.* Jyväskylä, Finland: PS-kustannus.

Hatcher, B. and Petty, K. (2004) "Visible thought in dramatic play." *Young Children*, November, 79–82.

Henderson, A. and Mapp, K. (2002) *A New Wave of Evidence: The Impact of School, Family, and Community Connections on Student Achievement.* Austin, TX: Southwest Educational Development Laboratory.

Hoffman, J. (2010) "Looking back and looking forward." *Childhood Education 87*, 1, 8–16.

Howell, J. and Corbey-Scullen, L. (1997) "Out of the housekeeping corner and onto the stage-extending dramatic play." *Young Children*, 52, 82–8.

Isbell, R. and Raines, S. (2007) *Creativity and the Arts with Young Children.* Clifton Park, NY: Thomson-Delmar Learning.

Isbell, R., Sobol, J., Lindauer, L., and Lowrance, A. (2004) "The effects of storytelling and story reading on the oral language complexity and story comprehension of young children." *Early Childhood Education Journal 32*, 3, 157–63.

Konishi, C. (2007) "Learning English as a second language." *Childhood Education 83*, 5, 267–72.

Lake, V. and Pappamihiel, N. (2003) "Effective practices and principles to support English language learners in the early childhood classroom." *Childhood Education 79*, 4, 200–203.

Logue, M., Robie, M., and Waite, K. (2009) "Read my dance: Promoting early writing through dance." *Childhood Education 85*, 4, 216–22.

McGee, L. (2003) "Book Acting, Storytelling and Drama in the Early Childhood Classroom." In D. Barone and L. Morrow (eds) *Research-Based Practices in Early Literacy.* New York, NY: Guilford Press.

McKeown, M. and Beck, I. (2006) "Encouraging Young Children's Language Interactions with Stories." In D. Dickinson and S. Neuman (eds) *Handbook of Early Literacy Research, Volume 2.* New York, NY: Guilford Press.

McMaster, J.C. (1998) "'Doing' literature: Using drama to build literacy." *The Reading Teacher 51*, 7, 574–84.

Mages, W. (2008) "Does creative drama promote language development in early childhood? A review of the methods and measures employed in the empirical literature." *Review of Educational Research 78*, 1, 124–52.

Martinez, M. (1993) "Motivating story reenactments." *The Reading Teacher 46*, 8, 682–8.

Morrow, L. (1990) "The impact of classroom environment changes to promote literacy during play." *Early Childhood Research Quarterly*, 5, 537–54.

Morrow, L. and Schickedanz, J. (2006) "The Relationships between Sociodramatic Play and Literacy Development." In D. Dickinson and S. Neuman (eds) *Handbook of Early Literacy Research, Volume 2.* New York, NY: Guilford Press.

Morrow, L. and Smith, J. (1990) "The effects of group size on interactive storybook reading." *Reading Research Quarterly*, 25, 213–231.

Moyer, J. (2001) "The child-centered kindergarten." *Childhood Education 77*, 3, 161–6.

National Reading Panel (2000) *Report of the National Reading Panel: Teaching Children to Read: An Evidence-Based Assessment of the Scientific Research Literature on Reading and its Implications for Reading Instruction.* Washington, DC: National Institute of Child Health and Human Development, National Institutes of Health.

Neuman, S. and Dickinson, D.K. (2001) *Handbook of Early Literacy Research.* New York, NY: Guilford Press.

Paley, V. (1990) *The Boy Who Would Be a Helicopter.* Chicago, IL: University of Chicago Press.

Paris, S. (2005) "Reinterpreting the development of reading skills." *Reading Research Quarterly 40*, 2, 184–202.

Pellegrini, A. and Galda, L. (1982) "The effects of thematic-fantasy play training on the development of children's story comprehension." *American Educational Research Journal*, 19, 443–52.

Pellegrini, A. and Galda, L. (1991) "Longitudinal Relations among Preschoolers' Play, Linguistic Verbs, and Emergent Literacy." In J. Christie (ed.) *Play and Early Literacy Development*. Albany, NY: SUNY Press.

Perlmutter, J., Folger, T., and Holt, K. (2009) "Pre-kindergartens learn to write." *Childhood Education 86*, l, 14–19.

Piaget, J. (1962) *Play, Dreams, and Imitation in Childhood*. New York, NY: W.W. Norton.

Podlozny, A. (2000) "Strengthening verbal skills through the use of classroom drama: A clear link." *Journal of Aesthetic Education 34*, 3–4, 239–75.

Porche, M. (2001) "Parent Involvement as a Link between Home and School." In D. Dickinson and P. Tabors (eds) *Beginning Literacy with Language: Young Children Learning at Home and in School.* Baltimore, MD: Brookes.

Raban, B. (2002) "Talking to Think, Learn, and Teach." In P. Smith (ed.). *Talking Classrooms: Shaping Children's Learning through Oral Language Instruction.* Newark, DE: International Reading Association.

Riojas-Cortez, M. (2001) "It's all about talking: Oral language development in a bilingual classroom." *Dimensions of Early Childhood 29*, 1, 11–l5.

Roskos, K., Christie, J., and Richgels, D. (2003) "The essentials of early literacy instruction." *Young Children 58*, 2, 52–60.

Roskos, K., Tabors, P., and Lenhart, L. (2004) *Oral Language and Early Literacy in Preschool: Talking, Reading, and Writing*. Newark, DE: International Reading Association.

Schomburg, R. (1996) "Using symbolic play abilities to assess academic readiness." National Association for the Education of Young Children Series, *Play, Policy, and Practice Connections*, 4, 1–3.

Smilansky, S. (1968) *The Effects of Sociodramatic Play on Disadvantaged Children*. New York, NY: Wiley.

Smilansky, S. and Shefatya, L. (1990) *Facilitating Play: A Medium for Promoting Cognitive, Socio-Emotional and Academic Development in Young Children*. Gaithersburg, MD: Psychological and Educational Publications.

Stone, S. and Chakraborty, B. (2011) "Classroom idea-sparkers." *Childhood Education 87*, 5, 7–8.

Strasser, J. and Seplocha, H. (2007) "Using picture books to support young children's literacy." *Childhood Education 83*, 4, 219–24.

Sulzby, E. (1985) "Children's emergent reading of favorite storybooks: A developmental study." *Reading Research Quarterly 20*, 4, 458–81.

Vygotsky, L. (1967) "Play and its role in the mental development of the child." *Soviet Psychology 6*, 3, 6–18.

Vygotsky, L. (1978; original work published in 1933) "The Role of Play in Development." In M. Cole, J. John-Steiner, S. Scribner, and E. Souberman (eds) *Mind in Society: The Development of Higher Psychological Process*. Cambridge, MA: Harvard University Press.

Vygotsky, L. (2004) "Imagination and creativity in childhood." *Journal of Russian and East European Psychology 42*, 1, 4–84. (Original work published in 1930.)

Wood, C. (1997) *Yardsticks: Children in the Classroom Ages 4–14*. Greenfield, MA: Northeast Foundation for Children.

Woodard, C. (1984) "Guidelines for facilitating sociodramatic play." *Childhood Education 60*, 3, 172–7.

Woodard, C. (1987) *Physical Science in Early Childhood*. Springfield, IL: Charles Thomas Publishers.

Woodard, C., Haskins, G., Schaefer, G., and Smolen, L. (2004) "Let's talk: A different approach to oral language development." *Young Children 59*, 4, 92–5.

Yau, M. (1992) "Drama: Its potential as a teaching and learning tool." *Scope Research Services 7*, 1, 3–6.

INDEX